W9-BKY-915

Homeland Security and
Counterterrorism Careers

# *Border Patrol Agent*

## *and Careers in Border Protection*

*by* Ann Graham Gaines

**Enslow Publishers, Inc.**
40 Industrial Road
Box 398
Berkeley Heights, NJ 07922
USA

http://www.enslow.com

**Library of Congress Cataloging-in-Publication Data**

Gaines, Ann Graham.
   Border patrol agent and careers in border protection / Ann Graham Gaines.
      p. cm. — (Homeland security and counterterrorism careers)
   Includes bibliographical references and index.
   ISBN 0-7660-2646-9
   1. Border patrol agents—United States—Juvenile literature. 2. Border patrol agents—Vocational guidance—United States—Juvenile literature. 3. Border patrols—United States—Juvenile literature. 4. U.S. Customs and Border Protection—Juvenile literature. I. Title. II. Series.

   JV6483.G35 2006
   363.28'502373—dc22

                              2006013273

Printed in the United States of America

10  9  8  7  6  5  4  3  2  1

**To Our Readers:**
We have done our best to make sure all Internet Addresses in this book were active and appropriate when we went to press. However, the author and the publisher have no control over and assume no liability for the material available on those Internet sites or on other Web sites they may link to. Any comments or suggestions can be sent by e-mail to comments@enslow.com or to the address on the back cover.

**Photo Credits:** Associated Press, AP, pp. 11, 84; Associated Press, U.S. Government, p. 9; CORBIS/Ali Jarekji/Reuters, p. 110; CORBIS SYGMA, p. 6; Getty Images, p. 89; Library of Congress, pp. 18, 19, 23; The Seattle Times/Benjamin Benschneider, p. 4; U.S. Customs and Border Protection, pp. 3, 25, 36; U.S. Customs and Border Protection/Charles Csavossy, p. 109; U.S. Customs and Border Protection/Gerald Nino, pp. 3, 35, 39, 40, 51, 53, 79, 99, 107; U.S. Customs and Border Protection/James R. Tourtellotte, pp. 1, 3, 13, 14, 15, 21, 30, 32–33, 34, 41, 43, 45, 46, 49, 54, 56, 57, 58, 60, 62, 63 (top and bottom), 64, 67, 68, 71, 72–73, 75, 77, 80, 82, 86, 91, 92–93, 94, 97, 100–101, 103, 104; U.S. Customs and Border Protection/University of Oklahoma, pp. 3, 16; U.S. Department of Agriculture photo, p. 26.

**Cover Photo:** U.S. Customs and Border Protection/James R. Tourtellotte

# Contents

Customs inspector Diana Dean makes a routine passenger check at the U.S. border. In 1999, Dean helped catch a dangerous criminal.

# Chapter 1

# *The Millennium Bomber*

It is 6:00 P.M. on December 14, 1999. At this time of year, it is already dark in Port Angeles in the state of Washington. Down at the docks, a ferryboat chugs up. It has come from Victoria. The port of Victoria is located just across the Strait of San Juan de Fuca in Canada. The ferry carries cars and trucks back and forth between the two ports.[1]

After driving off the ferry, the cars form a long line. When travelers go from one country to another, they must go through customs. Several customs inspectors work at the Port Angeles dock. One of these inspectors is Diana Dean. She has worked for the U.S. Customs Service for twenty-two years. This agency is part of the U.S. government.

Dean is almost at the end of her workday. All day long, she has been interviewing drivers, one by one. They drive up to her station. When they roll down their windows, she says hello. She asks them where they have come from. Where are they going? She wants to know if they have any goods to declare, or announce. (The law requires people to declare

This man used a fake passport when he tried to enter the United States in 1999. He said his name was Benni Noris.

certain things, such as alcoholic beverages or expensive jewelry, if they take the items from one country to another. This is because people must pay a special tax, or a duty, on them.) Dean is on a sharp lookout for criminals. She is also making sure people do not bring anything illegal or dangerous, such as guns or drugs, into the United States.

Finally, the last car comes off the ferry. Dean notices it is a fancy new car. She leans forward to talk to the driver. He is a young man. Dean asks to see his ID. He is originally from Algeria, a country in northern Africa. His passport says his name is Benni Noris and he is a citizen of Canada.

The passport looks real. So do Noris's driver's license and credit cards. Still, Dean worries. She notices that Noris is sweating. This seems strange. After all, it is freezing outside. He also acts very nervous. Dean asks the same questions she always does. Noris tells her he lives in Montreal. He is going to Seattle. It is taking him a very long time to answer questions. "Why are you going to Seattle?" Dean asks.

"To visit," he replies.

"Who are you going to visit?" she asks.

"A hotel," says Noris.[2]

Dean feels more and more suspicious. She acts on instinct—a gut feeling. She asks Noris to open his trunk.

The passport looks real.
So do Noris's driver's
license and credit
cards. Still, Dean
worries. She notices
that Noris is sweating.
This seems strange.

Looking back, she will later say, "I've done this a thousand times, maybe more, and couldn't tell you what I was looking for that day."[3]

At Dean's direction, Noris moves his car over to a parking space and gets out. After he unlocks the trunk, he stands next to the car. Inspectors are looking inside. Suddenly, Noris throws off his coat.

He takes off running, heading toward downtown. For five blocks, he runs "like a sprinter."[4] Customs officers are hot on his trail. He weaves around other pedestrians. He dashes across streets. When he reaches the small town's Main Street, he tries to steal a car. He flings open its door and forces out the driver. But before he can get inside, a customs inspector tackles him.

Back at the ferry crossing, Dean and the others are stunned. They have discovered twelve bags filled with

---

Later, scientists tested the powder and the liquid from Noris's car. He was carrying enormously powerful explosives.

---

white powder, two jars of yellow liquid, and four small black boxes hidden in Noris's trunk. When they open one box, they see a watch and a piece of a computer circuit board. There are wires all over it. All the inspectors know it is a timer for a bomb. They also have found a map of the Los Angeles airport. What does this mean? They fear the worst.[5]

Later, scientists tested the powder and the liquid from Noris's car. He was carrying enormously powerful explosives. These explosives have the capacity to blow a large building sky-high. Other

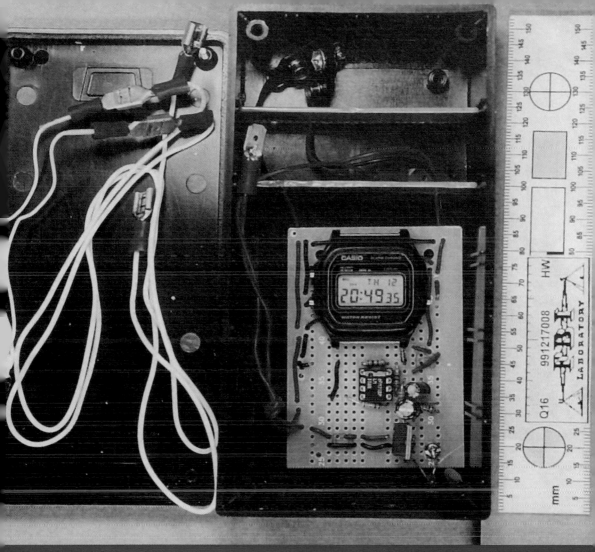

*Inspectors found this bomb timer in the trunk of Ressam's car. He planned to blow up the Los Angeles airport.*

investigators discover that Benni Noris is an assumed name. The man's real name is Ahmed Ressam. He is a terrorist. The French government has known for years that he is a dangerous man. Still, he has been able to avoid the police. A terrorist organization sent Ressam to North America. Their plan was for him to bomb the Los Angeles airport.

Ressam's arrest makes the news. Reporters give him the nickname Millennium Bomber. It is clear he hoped to attack on New Year's Eve while people celebrated the new millennium. Everybody praises Diana Dean. Her boss says that Dean's "experienced judgment, behavioral observation, and questioning techniques"[6] have helped her prevent what could have been a horrible tragedy.

Ressam goes on trial. In April 2001, a jury finds him guilty of terrorism and bomb smuggling. In prison, he gives investigators information about other terrorists living in North America. He tells them the names of people trained by Osama bin Ladin's al-Qaeda, a terrorist organization. It turns out that Dean has made one of the biggest busts of the century.

## CBP and Today's World

Just five months after Ressam received his sentence, hijackers crashed two airplanes into the World Trade Center in New York City. A third plane hit the Pentagon in Arlington, Virginia. Brave passengers fought the hijackers of a fourth plane. It crashed in a cornfield in Pennsylvania.

At that point, U.S. government officials knew beyond doubt that they needed to make the country a safer place. One thing Congress did was pass a law establishing a brand-new department in the federal

This is a courtroom sketch of Ahmed Ressam on April 6, 2001, the day he was convicted of terrorism.

government—the Department of Homeland Security. Inside Homeland Security, they put together several agencies. One that does very important work is called the U.S. Customs and Border Protection (CBP) agency.

Customs inspectors or agents, like Diana Dean, used to be part of the Customs Service. When CBP was founded, the Customs Service closed. Customs agents moved to CBP. They also received a new title. Today they are called CBP officers. Border Patrol agents and agriculture specialists now work for CBP, too.

As a group, CBP employees' number-one job is to protect the nation's borders. They keep out terrorists.

As a group, CBP employees' number-one job is to protect the nation's borders. They keep out terrorists. Yet there is a great deal more to their job. Border Patrol agents and CBP officers keep other kinds of criminals out of the United States. It is also their duty to catch illegal aliens—people who are not criminals but who try to come to work or live in the United States without the government's approval. It is also CBP officers' duty to check cargo that comes into the United States. They help the government collect duties on

Every year, CBP gives an award to the people who have done the most to fight terrorism. Its antiterrorism award is named after Diana Dean and Jose Melendez-Perez. As you know, Dean stopped the Millennium Bomber.

Melendez-Perez (above) is an immigration inspector. In August 2001, he was working at a Florida airport. A man named Mohamed al-Kahtani got off an airplane from Saudi Arabia. He did not have all the papers he needed to come into the United States.

Melendez-Perez questioned al-Kahtani. What did he plan to do here? Al-Kahtani first told him one story. Then he told another. Melendez-Perez decided that al-Kahtani was a threat. He sent him back to Saudi Arabia. Later, officials learned that one of the terrorists involved in the September 11 attacks had been at the airport to meet al-Kahtani.

In 2005, Anthony Jackson received the Diana Dean and Jose Melendez-Perez Anti-Terrorism Award. Jackson is a CBP official. He was working at the St. Paul/Minneapolis International Airport in Minnesota. One day, he stopped a passenger from the European city of Amsterdam. Jackson discovered that the man had papers describing plans to attack the United States and Great Britain.

## What It Takes

CBP has a tough job. It protects two borders. To the north lies a border 3,987 miles long. It separates the United States and Canada. To the south is the border with Mexico. It is 1,951 miles long. CBP also helps the U.S. Coast Guard protect 95,000 miles of U.S. shoreline.

What does it take to control the borders? On a typical day in 2005, CBP workers interviewed 1 million people who wanted to enter the United States. They inspected 65,000 truck, rail, and ship containers. They checked about 365,000 passenger cars and trucks. To do their jobs, CBP workers themselves drove 13,400 cars and trucks. They used 400 all-terrain vehicles (ATVs), 130 horses, 85 aircraft, and 75 boats.

By the end of this typical day, CBP had seized 210 phony documents. They had sent home 1,343 people who tried to enter the country illegally. And they had arrested one person who threatened U.S. safety.[7]

goods being brought into the country. They also work to keep out restricted or illegal items, such as the kind of uranium used to build deadly nuclear bombs.

Working at CBP requires special training. Border Patrol agents and CBP officers need to be smart and alert. On the job, they use all kinds of high-tech equipment, vehicles, and weapons. If you think Diana Dean's story is interesting, a career with this government agency may provide an exciting path for your future.

With some special training, you could become a Border Patrol agent or a CBP officer. These CBP officers are doing a routine inspection of a plane and its cargo.

The Customs Service was the first agency founded to protect U.S. borders. This picture was taken in the 1880s.

# Chapter 2

# A Short History of Customs and Border Protection

CBP is a new government agency. It was founded in 2003—but its history goes back much further. CBP took over many of the duties of four other agencies: the Customs Service, the Immigration and Naturalization Service, the Border Patrol, and the Department of Agriculture.

## The Customs Service

George Washington was president when the U.S. Customs Service was founded in 1789. This makes it one of the very first government agencies. Why was the Customs Service founded? In its very early years, the U.S. government was poor. After the American Revolution (1775–1783), the government owed money. Other countries and individuals had helped pay for the war. The United States needed money to pay them back. Congress passed laws allowing the U.S. Treasury to collect duties on imports—goods being brought into the country for sale.

Congress created the Customs Service to collect these duties. The service included fifty-nine customs districts in eleven states. Every district had its own agents. Washington chose men he trusted to be the agents. Many had fought with him in the Revolution. The agents had offices in Customs Houses, usually located at ports. The busiest houses were in the cities of Boston, Philadelphia, New York, and Baltimore. All of these

*In the 1800s, trading ships like this clipper ship had to pay duties on goods they brought into the United States. It was the Customs Service's job to collect the duties.*

*When people began to enter the country by plane, customs agents collected duties at airports, too.*

cities had harbors, where sailing ships put down their anchors. Ships came from faraway places—Caribbean islands, Europe, and even Africa.

At the Customs Houses, agents registered and licensed ships. They looked at ships' cargo lists to see what they carried. They collected duties for the government. Their work also took them to the ports' docks. There they checked vessels to confirm what they were carrying. They also inspected ships about to sail to other countries. Ship owners had to pay duties on some exports, or goods being shipped out of the United States for sale in other countries.

Over the years, the duties the Customs Service collected helped the nation grow. The money helped buy the Louisiana Territory, Florida, Oregon, and Alaska. As the country grew, new customs districts were created. By the mid-1800s, there were Customs Houses on the Great Lakes, in Texas, and in California. By 1900, thousands of customs inspectors were on the job. This number grew again when people began to travel by airplane in the 1920s. Customs agents began working at airports as well as seaports.[1]

## The Immigration and Naturalization Service

For a long time, the U.S. government was most worried about *what* came into the country. In time, it also wanted to control *who* came into the country. After the Civil War (1861–1865), the number of immigrants increased rapidly. Immigrants are people who come from one country into another to live. At first, the U.S. government did not try to limit the number of immigrants who came, with one exception. Congress passed laws limiting the number of Chinese people who could come to the United States. During the Gold Rush, American miners feared Chinese workers would take their jobs and drive down wages.

Immigration laws changed in 1891. That year, Congress passed the Immigration Act. It limited who could come to the United States. It created the new Immigration Service. Immigration stations opened all

## Smuggling

Smugglers are people who sneak something into a country illegally. Sometimes smugglers bring in illegal goods. Other times they attempt to bring legal goods into the country without paying a duty. In the nineteenth century, customs agents were on the lookout for ships carrying more containers of molasses than the ship's captain had declared.

Today, most smugglers are trying to bring illegal drugs into the United States. They also hide jewels, weapons, and money. Others sneak in computer software and pirated CDs and DVDs. Some smugglers even try to bring in valuable artwork, which they hope to sell.

In 2003, during the war in Iraq, archaeological sites and the Iraqi National Museum were looted. Precious items stolen from these sites were smuggled into the United States. American customs officials recovered some of the priceless objects, but thousands of pieces of art and artifacts have yet to be found.[2]

over the United States. The biggest and busiest was at Ellis Island in New York Harbor. Every day, thousands of immigrants came on steamships from Europe to New York. Other big stations were located in Chicago, in San Francisco, and in El Paso and San Antonio, Texas.

At Ellis Island, as at other stations, doctors checked immigrants as soon as they arrived. Some had serious diseases, such as tuberculosis. They were sent back to their homelands. Next, immigration inspectors questioned the people who passed the medical exam. The inspectors checked people's names and home countries. They asked questions to find out what they planned to do in the United States. Their job was to keep out criminals. They also kept out people who had no money and people who seemed unlikely to find work.

For close to forty years, the Immigration Service was part of the Department of the Treasury. In 1933, President Franklin Delano Roosevelt made it a separate agency. It got a new name: the Immigration and Naturalization Service. In 1940, it became part of the Department of Justice.

For the rest of the twentieth century, the Immigration and Naturalization Service was responsible for immigrants who came to the United States. Immigration officials took care of paperwork for foreigners who arrived by car, bus, train, boat, or airplane to live in the United States. Another part of their job was to look for illegal aliens. These are people who do not have the legal right to live or work in the United States.[3]

*Immigrants at Ellis Island finish up their paperwork so they can enter the United States. Ellis Island was one of the main ports of entry on the East Coast.*

## The Border Patrol

Immigration officials worked at ports of entry. For years, however, no one regularly patrolled U.S. borders. This changed in 1924. That year, the Border Patrol was founded. Its job was to catch people trying to sneak into the country. In the beginning, the Border Patrol was part of the Department of Labor. Later it became part of the Immigration and Naturalization Service.

At first, Border Patrol agents worked mostly on the U.S.–Mexico border. There were only a few workers assigned to the Canadian border. The first agents did most of their work on foot or on horseback. Even today, agents still travel this way if they go into the wilderness. Over time, some Border Patrol agents began to use trucks. In the late twentieth century, the agency also began to use ATVs and helicopters.

In the beginning, a major job for the Border Patrol was to stop people from sneaking alcohol into the United States. (Alcohol was outlawed in the United States from 1919 to 1933.) Agents also enforced laws that kept out Chinese immigrants. Later, the government wanted to control how many Mexican people came into the country. More and more Border Patrol agents were assigned to the southern border during the 1980s and 1990s. At that time, there was a great increase in the number of illegal aliens who tried to come in from Mexico.

## The Department of Agriculture

At first, the U.S. government did not worry about plants that people brought into the country. Scientists knew about plant diseases, but there were no federal

*Early Border Patrol agents used cars to patrol the U.S.–Mexico border in Del Rio, Texas.*

laws regulating plant imports until the twentieth century. In 1912, Congress passed the Plant Quarantine Act. The U.S. Department of Agriculture hired inspectors. They examined plants and produce brought into the United States. They watched for diseased plants. They also inspected plants, fruits, and vegetables to make sure they were not carrying pests. (Pests are insects that carry diseases that hurt plants.) By the late twentieth century,

Department of Agriculture employees inspect the packages of travelers returning to El Paso, Texas, from Juarez, Mexico, in 1937.

the Department of Agriculture had thousands of agriculture specialists. When CBP was founded in 2003, these inspectors moved to the new agency.[4]

## Terrorism Requires Changes

By the mid-twentieth century, the three large agencies that would end up as CBP—the Border Patrol, the Customs Service, and the Immigration and Naturalization Service—were established. Their duties were clear. The Department of Agriculture's plant-inspection program was also in place. The focus of all of these agencies changed when the U.S. government became more concerned about terrorism.

The U.S. government defines terrorism like this: "the unlawful use of—or threatened use of—force or violence against individuals or property to coerce or intimidate governments or societies, often to achieve political, religious, or ideological objectives."[5]

Acts of terrorism are carefully planned. Their purpose is to force a government to do something. For example, terrorists might plan an attack to force a country to free certain prisoners. Their targets may be government buildings. Terrorists also hurt people. Usually, it is regular people (civilians) rather than members of the military who are hurt. An army does not carry out terrorism. Instead, small groups of people with a common goal become terrorists.

Many Americans may think terrorism is a new problem. In reality, terrorism began thousands of years

## Target: Nuclear Triggers

CBP officers go through special training to learn to recognize materials that might be parts of weapons of mass destruction. In 1990, customs agents helped retrieve forty nuclear trigger devices called krytrons. A company with an office in Great Britain ordered the triggers. The order seemed perfectly legal. A Customs Service investigation found vital information, however. The office was run by a company in Iraq. It planned to ship the krytrons to terrorists in that country. The U.S. supplier had no idea about the Iraqi connection. CBP employees remain on the lookout for dangerous items.[6]

ago. We also tend to think of it as a problem that comes from the Middle East. In truth, acts of terrorism have been carried out all over the world. Terrorists are people of many nationalities.

The term *terrorism* comes from a French word, *terrorisme*. It was first used during the French Revolution (1789–1794). At that time, France had a divided society. Some people were extremely rich, others extremely poor. The poor were unhappy about how they were treated. During the revolution, citizens overthrew the government. A new government declared the king, Louis XVI, guilty of crimes against the people. He was put to death. The government then ruled mostly by frightening people into obedience. It used terror to bring change to the country.

By the twentieth century, rebels plotted to overthrow governments in many parts of the world. In 1914, Serbian nationalists wanted to take back Serbia. This country had been taken over by the Austro-Hungarian Empire. With this goal in mind, a man named Gavrilo Princip assassinated Archduke Ferdinand of Austria. This act of terrorism helped lead to World War I (1914–1918).

In the late twentieth century there was a surge in terrorist activity. The Irish Republican Army launched violent attacks. It hoped the attacks might

In 1914, Serbian nationalists wanted to take back Serbia. Gavrilo Princip assassinated Archduke Ferdinand of Austria. This helped lead to World War I.

lead to Ireland's freedom from English rule. Other acts of terror have been tied to problems in Israel. There, Jews occupy an area of land that Arab Palestinians believe is theirs. People around the world disagree about who has the right to this land. Some Palestinians believe Israelis have stolen it. They are willing to die—and to murder—to reclaim

The Department of Homeland Security (DHS) was created in November 2001. Here, President Bush thanks DHS employees for their hard work.

it. In turn, Israelis have been willing to use violence against Palestinians to protect what they believe is theirs.

Americans also became more worried about terrorism. In 1993, terrorists tried to blow up the World Trade Center in New York City. In 1995, an American named Timothy McVeigh drove a truck filled with explosives up to the Alfred P. Murrah Federal Building in Oklahoma City. When the truck exploded, it brought down much of the building. The attack killed 168 people, including 19 children.

These were frightening events. Yet it was the events of September 11, 2001, that truly terrified the nation. Until then, it seemed impossible that large numbers of Americans could be attacked on their own soil. The planes that crashed into the World Trade Center and the Pentagon proved that terrorism could strike anytime, anywhere.

## The Department of Homeland Security

To fight terrorism, President George W. Bush signed the Homeland Security Act in November 2001. This law created the Department of Homeland Security, known as the DHS. In the months that followed, there were major changes in government agencies involved in protecting Americans from terrorist threats. One of the new agencies that became part of the DHS was the U.S. Customs and Border Protection agency. The Border Patrol, Customs

*Several government agencies were combined to create the DHS. Their goal was never to let a terrorist attack like September 11 happen again.*

Service, Immigration and Naturalization Service, and Department of Agriculture were all reorganized.

The Border Patrol became part of CBP. The Department of Agriculture's plant quarantine program also became part of CBP. Some customs agents and immigration officials were assigned to the new agency. Others went to work for another new agency called U.S. Immigration and Customs Enforcement. CBP was

formally in service on March 1, 2003. It moved into headquarters on Pennsylvania Avenue in Washington, D.C., near the White House.

From the beginning, CBP was a huge agency. In 2006 it had more than forty-two thousand employees. Thirty thousand of these employees work in law enforcement.[7] This means their job is to make sure the nation's laws are followed. According to Robert C. Bonner,

CBP officers protect a busy port on the front lines of homeland security.

former CBP commissioner, CBP is "by far the largest law enforcement agency of the federal government."[8]

CBP's law enforcement staff is organized into three groups: Border Patrol agents, CBP officers, and agricultural specialists. They all work on the front line. (We say people are on the front line when they are in especially important positions or in a dangerous place, like a battlefront.) The agency's other twelve thousand employees assist CBP's frontline employees in various ways. They are called support staff. Together, CBP's employees work hard to build on the history of border protection.

## Hurricane Katrina

Hurricane Katrina struck part of the U.S. coast of the Gulf of Mexico in August 2005. It damaged 90,000 square miles of land in four states. More than one thousand Americans died. One million more were forced from their homes. The DHS stepped in to help. Its agencies and their employees were needed in the recovery effort. CBP offered its support. Some 650 CBP volunteers were on hand to help in this time of great need.

CBP workers gathered equipment and supplies. Then CBP helicopter pilots took the supplies to people who needed them. They also took electrical generators to shelters in Louisiana and Mississippi.[9] In New Orleans, CBP pilots rescued victims from the Superdome and from flooded neighborhoods.

Teams of CBP workers led searches for missing people. They rode with local law enforcement. They helped respond to calls for help. They provided security and helped stop looting and theft. CBP workers handed out food and rescued people. They cut down trees and repaired homes. They helped people find lost property. Sadly, they also helped recover the dead.

After the storm, CBP's commissioner at the time, Robert Bonner, remarked on how his agency's employees had served the nation. "Our volunteer CBP rescue workers saved lives and eased suffering in this time of great need," he said. "Their effort, dedication and sacrifice in my eyes have been heroic."[10]

The work of a Border Patrol agent is exciting and difficult. Here, agents participate in a fast rope exercise to get out of a helicopter quickly.

# Chapter 3

# Working as a Border Patrol Agent

Border Patrol agents have an important job. Their number-one task is to stop terrorists and weapons from getting into the United States. They keep people from bringing drugs and other illegal items across the border. It is also their job to keep illegal aliens from sneaking into the country.[1]

Border Patrol agents work along the northern and southern borders. Only rarely does their work take them into other parts of the country. Most Border Patrol jobs are in Texas, New Mexico, Arizona, and California. Agents work in smaller numbers in the states along the northern border.

Border Patrol agents are assigned to sector offices. They spend only some of their time in the office, though. That is where they catch up on paperwork or meet with their bosses. Most of their workday is spent out of the office.

Sometimes Border Patrol agents work at checkpoints. Some border checkpoints are permanent. They have a building and a parking lot or booths where

> Border Patrol agents stop every car and truck that arrives. They talk to the drivers. They ask basic questions about where they are going.

drivers stop. Others are temporary. To set up a temporary checkpoint, agents pick out one stretch of highway. They pull squad cars out in the middle of the road. Then they stop all traffic. They might do this for several hours. Then they move on to another place. This allows agents to catch people who are in the country without permission. In the past, almost all checkpoints were in the Southwest. This is changing. More and more checkpoints are now along the U.S.–Canadian border.

The process is the same at both types of checkpoint. Border Patrol agents stop every car and truck that arrives. They talk to the drivers. They ask basic questions about where they are going. The agents must work quickly. They check people's papers and ask to see a driver's license. For people who are not U.S. citizens, the agents check a tourist visa, a work card, or another photo ID. Agents are specially trained to recognize fake or forged papers. When they find illegal aliens, agents detain them. This means the people are put in custody. Unless they can prove there has been a mistake, they are sent back to their homeland. At checkpoints, Border Patrol agents also look at what cars and trucks are carrying. They always watch for

These CBP officers are reviewing the papers of someone crossing a border. They are checking for suspicious or fake documents.

containers that might be transporting drugs. Anything unusual may alert agents that something is not right. Here is an example of such a case. In November 2003, *The Press Enterprise*, a California newspaper, reported

*Checkpoint agents ask every driver questions. They also scan the car for anything unusual.*

that Border Patrol agents captured a drug smuggler. At first, the agents at the checkpoint noticed nothing wrong. Then they saw a man come through with forty huge cans of hominy in the back of his truck. (Hominy is a special kind of corn.) That was all he was carrying—a year's supply of hominy. This was strange enough. But the agents definitely knew something was wrong when they asked him what was in the cans. He did not say he was carrying hominy. He said he had jalapeño peppers. That is when they brought in a drug-sniffing dog. All of those cans were packed with marijuana.[2]

When they are not in their office or at a checkpoint, Border Patrol agents do the line watch. This means they go out on patrol to check out one stretch of border. Sometimes they do this in trucks or SUVs.

Other times they mount horses or go out on ATVs. This allows them to travel off-road. Other Border Patrol agents go into the wilderness or desert on foot to try to catch illegal aliens. Recently, the federal government purchased new boats for the patrol to use, especially in California and Washington State.

Sometimes agents on patrol run into people crossing the border illegally. Other times they are following a lead from an informant, or witness. Sometimes people who live on the border see people

*On their ATVs, Border Patrol agents can reach places far away from major roads.*

sneaking across their land. Surveillance equipment also provides leads.

One special tool the Border Patrol uses is the Integrated Surveillance Intelligence System (ISIS). ISIS has cameras that can be used remotely, or from a distance. The cameras take pictures in dark or light. ISIS also has sensors that can detect a person crossing the border.[3] Law enforcement communications assistants monitor the videos and data that ISIS provides. If agents learn that there has been a crossing, they go out to find the person who has crossed the border. A necessary skill Border Patrol agents learn is tracking. This allows them to follow footprints, tire tracks, and other clues to find people in hiding.

## What It Is Like to Work for the Border Patrol

A Border Patrol agent's job can be extremely difficult.[4] An agent almost never works what most Americans consider a regular workweek, from 8:00 A.M. to 5:00 P.M. Monday through Friday. Every office has agents on duty twenty-four hours a day. Other agents are on call, which means they carry a cell phone or a pager with them at all times. They can be called in whenever they are needed. Agents take turns working on weekends and holidays. Border Patrol agents also work a lot of overtime. Most put in close to fifty hours per week. (The typical full-time workweek in the United States is forty hours.)

CBP agents have to work many hours each week.
They can be called to the job on a moment's notice.

Agents work under difficult conditions. From time to time, they go on overnight stakeouts. Their work also takes them outdoors in all kinds of weather. On the country's southern border, the heat gets very intense, especially in the summer. Up north, agents must deal with snow and ice. Near Canada, the temperature often falls well below zero. The job is physically demanding, too. Sometimes agents have to run a long way. On chases, they may have to climb cliffs or jump from walls. Checkpoint agents need to be on their feet for hours at a time.

In August 2005, a group
of illegal aliens
threw so many rocks
at a Border Patrol
helicopter that it was
forced to land.

An agent's job is also stressful. Border Patrol agents sometimes find themselves in danger. Drug runners often carry guns, for example. And in August 2005, a group of illegal aliens threw so many rocks at a Border Patrol helicopter that it was forced to land.

More often, agents find themselves confronting a sad situation. Many of the Mexican workers they arrest truly need work. Mexico is a poor country without

*Customs officers carry a heavy load of seized marijuana in the hot desert. Their working conditions can be difficult.*

enough jobs. Many of its people have a hard time supporting their families. This is why so many come to the United States illegally. Border Patrol agents understand this, yet they are sworn to uphold the law. They must not let illegal aliens cross the border, even if those aliens have a good reason for wanting to come to the United States.

There is another thing that is hard on agents. Sometimes out in the desert, they come across people who are suffering from thirst or heat. Other times they open a truck trailer to find it crammed with illegal

## Border Rescues

When the CBP's Border Patrol
Search Trauma and Rescue
(BORSTAR) team heads into
the desert, it hopes to save
lives. Illegal aliens are often
so determined to get into the
United States that they take big
risks. Sometimes a "coyote" loads
people onto a railroad car or a
truck trailer in the heat of the summer.
(A coyote is a person paid to smuggle illegal aliens
across the border.) Other times, aliens strike out on their
own or with a group. They hope to cross hundreds of
miles of blazing-hot desert on foot.

In July 2005, a group of twenty-three illegal aliens
from Mexico became lost in the Arizona desert. One
was carrying a cell phone and called 911. The Pima
County Sheriff's Office called in the BORSTAR team.
At one point, they could no longer get in touch with
the man on his cell phone. The BORSTAR trackers
searched the area for hours, seeking signs of the group.
Finally, just as the sun was going down, they spotted
signal fires. Fortunately, no one was seriously hurt, but
they needed water badly.

Over and over again, the BORSTAR team is called
on to rescue illegal aliens who get lost or find themselves
trapped in a railcar or truck. In a single ten-month
period, BORSTAR rescued 722 people.[5] In one year,
BORSTAR teams and Mexican law enforcement
officials together saved nearly two thousand people.

aliens. People die trying to get over the border. This is one of the hardest parts of a Border Patrol agent's job.

Border Patrol agents can suffer great frustration. Sometimes their job feels like an impossible one. They know there will never be enough agents to patrol the entire border. Every month, agents in the town of Temecula, California, arrest hundreds of illegal aliens and seize drug shipments. Of course they are proud.

Agent Juan Estacuy said he has to accept that this is all they can do: "You don't change the world in one day, but little by little it helps."

Yet in the words of a local reporter, "No one believes that [this] represents a majority or even a significant dent in the overall flow of human beings and narcotics."[6] Agent Juan Estacuy said he has to accept that this is all they can do: "You don't change the world in one day, but little by little it helps."[7]

Think about Agent Estacuy's words. You will realize that even though a Border Patrol agent's job is difficult, it can also be rewarding. Many agents say they would not trade their job for any other. Why? First and foremost, it makes them proud to know they keep their country safe. They like knowing they work for justice. It is exciting for agents to arrest criminals. They feel pride when they stop a large drug shipment from getting across the border. Border Patrol agents are highly respected by other law enforcement officials. Agents prize that respect. They also value what they call their esprit de corps. This means that there is a great feeling of team spirit among Border Patrol agents. Agents are intensely loyal to one another. They protect each other.

Agents also appreciate the variety of their work. Border Patrol agents work inside and outside. One day they may go to work in a truck. Other days they will be on horseback or on a four-wheeler. And think of all the different people they meet.

Other advantages include an agent's pay and benefits. Border Patrol agents earn better money than local police officers do. Agents at the entry level earn a base salary of $34,000 per year. Those with more education or skills earn $38,700.[8] They are paid more for overtime work. Overtime pay can amount to another $10,000 every year. Agency employees have secure jobs. After a probationary period, an employee is guaranteed employment. CBP agents do not have to wonder whether they will be rehired from year to year.

The Border Patrol has a good promotion system, too. This means that as agents learn new skills and gain experience, they are assigned to higher-level jobs. That means they receive higher salaries.

*A CBP Cessna airplane patrols the southeastern United States. Keeping people safe makes CBP employees proud.*

As a final benefit, Border Patrol agents retire early. Agents can leave with full retirement benefits after twenty-five years of service. Retirement from the Border Patrol is required at age fifty-seven.

## Qualifications

Who can apply for a job as a Border Patrol agent? The job is open to people born in the United States. People born in another country can also apply, as long as they are U.S. citizens. Not all U.S. citizens qualify for the job, however. In 2005, citizens who lived outside of the United States could not qualify for a CBP job. Applicants had to have lived in the United States, a U.S. protectorate, or a U.S. territory for the last three years. (An example of a protectorate is the U.S. Virgin Islands.

To qualify for the Border Patrol agent job, candidates must have either a four-year college degree or a lot of job experience.

Territories include American Samoa and Guam.) There was one exception: people who had been working for the government overseas. Their spouses and children could also apply.[9]

To qualify for the Border Patrol agent job, candidates must have either a four-year college degree or a lot of job experience. Candidates do not need a college major in law enforcement. Many colleges have a major in border studies, for example. Such study is useful for a job with the Border Patrol.

There are age limits for the Border Patrol agent job. Candidates must be at least twenty-one and cannot be older than thirty-seven. There are also physical

## Surveillance Equipment

The Border Patrol relies on many kinds of surveillance equipment to keep an eye on the areas it patrols. It uses helicopters, planes, tower-mounted video cameras, ground sensors, and night-vision goggles. Recently it started to use an unmanned aerial vehicle (UAV). A UAV looks like a large remote-controlled model airplane. It has no pilot onboard. It is piloted by a person from a remote location.

A UAV was first used in the summer of 2004. This UAV was the single-engine Israeli-built Hermes 450 model. It can remain in the air for up to twenty hours. It cruises at 91 miles per hour (mph) but can reach speeds up to 125 mph. The Border Patrol usually flies the Hermes at 9,500 feet, but it can fly up to 18,000 feet.

The Border Patrol's UAV is equipped with image-recognition systems and sensors. These can detect movement, read a license plate number, and even

identify vehicle occupants from fifteen miles away. Infrared sensors provide day and night images. The UAV led to the capture of forty-two illegal aliens in just a few months.[10]

requirements. Border Patrol agents have to be able to see for long distances, so they must have good distance vision. They also have to be in great physical shape.

## Applying

Often there are no new Border Patrol jobs available. From time to time, though, CBP does need agents. It then posts an announcement on its Web site and lists the jobs on the federal government's official job site.

People may apply for the job online. After they apply, candidates make an appointment to take a written test. This test takes between four and five hours. One part of the test checks applicants' reasoning skills. This shows how good people are at solving puzzles. Another part deals with job-related experiences and achievements. Applicants also take a test in Spanish. If they do not know any Spanish, they are given what is called an artificial language test. This test can predict a person's ability to learn a new language.

People who get high scores on the test have an oral interview. If they do well, they undergo a background check. This is a search for criminal or drug arrests, job dismissals, excessive use of alcohol, any use of illegal drugs, and debts. All candidates must take a drug test. CBP workers often have to take charge of seized drugs, money, and valuables. It is especially important that people who work for the agency be honest and trustworthy.[11]

CBP officer trainees participate in their final physical training test. They have to keep in good shape.

Candidates also must have a medical exam. A trainer evaluates their fitness. All Border Patrol agents must be able to do twenty push-ups and twenty-five sit-ups, each in under one minute. They also must pass a step test, going up and down thirty stairs per minute for a five-minute stretch.

It is only after they have passed all the written tests, the background check, and the fitness test that candidates are offered a job.

*New Border Patrol agents train for five months before they start their jobs.*

## Training

Once hired, all new Border Patrol agents are sent away for five months of training. Training takes place at the Border Patrol Academy in Artesia, New Mexico. The days are full at the academy. One Border Patrol agent named Pedro Infante, who came from the U.S. Army, looked back at his training. He thought it was even "tougher than Army boot camp."[12]

At the Border Patrol Academy, new recruits spend hundreds of hours in the classroom. They take classes in immigration and criminal law. They learn about psychology. Everybody also takes Spanish classes. They drill in the language until they all speak Spanish fluently. Recruits who grew up speaking Spanish at home sometimes complain about taking Spanish classes. But CBP wants everybody to know the same slang as well as important legal terms.

Spanish teachers also spend time talking about Latin-American culture. Instructor Rich Plaatje believes this helps agents on the job. For example, he teaches his students that when they round up a group of illegal aliens, they should try to get "the oldest male to buy into your agenda."[13] This is because in Mexico, Guatemala, and other Latino countries, older people command great respect. They can influence a group.

Some people think the Border Patrol Academy's class work is hard. Others say it is not so bad. But everybody agrees that the physical training is tough. *Really* tough. The Border Patrol already knows its new recruits are fit. After all, they had to pass several tests to get the job. But at the academy, they double-check to make sure that all agents can run fast and for a long time. New recruits train until they can run 1.5 miles in less than 13 minutes. They have to do a 220-yard dash in less than 46 seconds. To get them ready for chases, trainees are also put through an obstacle course. They take special driving classes and learn how to shoot and take care of their firearms.

An agent faces the challenge of rappelling down a wall.

Once they finish their training, Border Patrol agents start their job. At first, everybody is assigned to a Border Patrol unit in California, New Mexico, Arizona, or Texas. Non-Spanish-speaking, married Border Patrol agents say that moving their families to rural locations where most families speak Spanish can be difficult.[14]

New Border Patrol agents do not have to start work on their own right away. First they are assigned to a field-training officer. They get one day of training per week. Border Patrol agents also have many opportunities for on-the-job training throughout their career. They learn special Border Patrol skills. They also learn many aspects of other CBP employees' jobs. Border Patrol agents thrive on being right on the front line of keeping their country safe.

## Weaponry and Training

Border Patrol agents and CBP officers sometimes find themselves in danger. They need to carry weapons. Border Patrol agents are armed with .40-caliber handguns, collapsible riot batons, and pepper spray. In special circumstances, they use shotguns or automatic rifles. CBP employees on the front line go through weapons training when they join the agency and must practice throughout their careers.

One thing Border Patrol agents find especially useful in their training is the Range 3000. It is like a life-size interactive video game. Agents enter a special trailer armed with fake weapons. Inside, they face

what look like real people in the act of committing a crime—for example, smuggling something illegal into the country. This gives agents a chance to practice what they would do in dangerous situations. The Range 3000 gives agents a chance to find out what it is like to be in a stressful situation. It also helps them learn when—and when not—to fire their weapons.[15]

CBP officers guard ports of entry throughout the United States.

# Chapter 4

# *The Job of a CBP Officer*

U.S. Customs and Border Protection officers are called CBP officers for short. CBP officers mostly do work that once was done by customs agents. They are also trained to do agricultural and immigration inspections. CBP's John McKay is in charge of training. He says it is tough to learn three jobs. He is confident in his personnel, however, saying, "They can do it."[1]

CBP officers work at 317 official ports of entry.[2] There is at least one port of entry in every state. There are also ports of entry in the District of Columbia, Puerto Rico, and the Virgin Islands. Some states have more ports of entry than others. States on the country's borders have many. For example, Texas has twenty-seven and California has twenty. North Dakota, with the long stretch of border it shares with Canada, also has twenty. On the other hand, Nebraska, located right in the middle of the United States, has just one. CBP also has fourteen pre-clearance offices in Canada and the Caribbean. CBP officers at these offices check passengers and cargo before they head for the United States.

This CBP officer uses new fingerprint technology to check an airplane passenger.

Many ports of entry are located at airports. Some of them are huge international airports where international flights land. Others are service airports where only cargo planes arrive. There are also ports of entry at seaports on the Atlantic Ocean, the Pacific Ocean, the Gulf of Mexico, and the Great Lakes. Some ports of entry serve people who come in trucks and cars from Mexico and Canada. One example is the port of entry at Laredo, Texas.

People coming from other countries—including immigrants, students, and tourists—have their official

Border Patrol Agent

papers checked at ports of entry. Importers and exporters go to ports of entry for the papers they need to ship goods into or out of the United States.

## The CBP Officer Job

A CBP officer's job is to check people and cargo coming into the United States. They enforce hundreds of customs, immigration, and agriculture laws. Their most important job is to keep out terrorists and terrorist weapons. In addition, they check to make sure that people coming into the country have valid passports or visas. They verify that the right forms have

> A CBP officer's job is to check people and cargo coming into the United States. Their most important job is to keep out terrorists and terrorist weapons.

been filled out for cargo. They look for drugs and other illegal items. Another important task is to collect duties. In 2004, CBP officers collected $27 billion in duties for the government.[3]

The work of a CBP officer varies according to where he or she is assigned. At airports, passengers who come off international flights get in line. When they

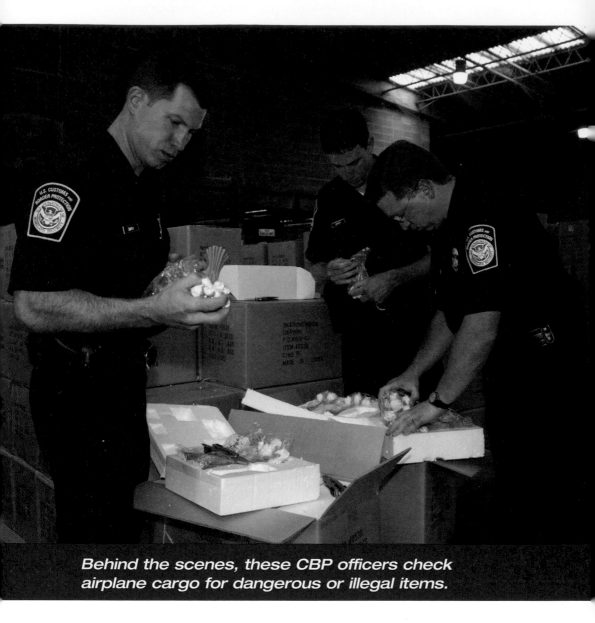

*Behind the scenes, these CBP officers check airplane cargo for dangerous or illegal items.*

reach a CBP officer in a booth or at a desk, they are interviewed. CBP officers check their papers. They verify that the papers are valid. People sometimes try to sneak into the United States using fake passports.

## Chemical and Biological Weapons

Countries around the world worry about biological and chemical weapons. Biological warfare means poisoning or infecting the public with a disease. Anthrax, a deadly bacterium, is an example of a biological weapon. By spreading anthrax, an enemy could kill large numbers of people because of the sickness it causes. Chemical warfare kills an enemy by spreading a toxin or poison through the air. Sarin gas, for example, can be spread using a missile or even a crop-duster airplane.

One of CBP's major goals is to prevent the use of these especially dangerous weapons. CBP officers, Border Patrol agents, and agriculture specialists are all trained to recognize them.

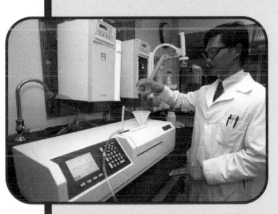

What happens when one is found? Seven CBP field offices have a Fast Response Team. Each team is made up of two, three, or four chemists who speed to crime scenes to collect evidence. Back in the lab, they use special equipment to find out the identity of the person who planted a chemical device. They also study the weapon itself.[4]

An officer may also check the bags a passenger carries. (Other CBP officers or Transportation Security Administration officers inspect checked baggage, which is handled by airline personnel.) Sometimes people bring in surprising things. Recently, a CBP officer opened a man's suitcase at the Los Angeles airport. Out flew a bird of paradise. The man was also trying to sneak in two monkeys—in his pants. People often try to smuggle in rare birds' eggs, which can be sold for

This CBP officer interviews a man arriving in the United States. It is her job to be both professional and friendly.

thousands of dollars. Sometimes they want to bring in tiger bones, which are used in traditional Chinese medicine. Tigers are endangered animals, so the bones cannot be sold in the United States. Other times they

> CBP officers tell stories of people eating smoked bats in front of them, to prove they can indeed be eaten.

want to bring in exotic foods. CBP officers tell stories of people eating smoked bats in front of them, to prove they can indeed be eaten.[5]

Today, some CBP officers work at pre-clearance stations in airports outside of the United States. These are located in Canada, the Caribbean, and Ireland. At pre-clearance stations, CBP officers have a special responsibility. The Federal Bureau of Investigation (FBI) identifies people who pose a security threat to the United States. CBP officers look for these people. There are two good reasons to keep dangerous people from boarding an airplane bound for the United States. First, it lowers the chance of hijacking—when someone tries to take over a plane. Second, it means the U.S. government does not have to pay to detain or deport (send away) a suspicious person.

Some people from other countries enter the United States by ship or train. CBP officers check people at seaports. They also inspect passenger trains. CBP officers mostly check cargo at seaports and train stations. There can be hundreds of cargo containers on a single freight train. Cargo ships carry thousands of containers. In the past, customs inspectors had to open cargo containers one by one to see what they carried. Sometimes they still look in a boxcar or go down into a ship's hold to inspect it.

Today, though, many inspections are done using amazing new technology. CBP has large X-ray and gamma-imaging systems. Officers use them to see what is inside cargo containers without having to open them. To examine containers carried on ships, they use the Eagle Mobile Sea Container X-ray System. This huge piece of equipment weighs 180,000 pounds. It allows officers to look through steel walls a foot thick.[6]

CBP officers also use $1.5 million gamma-ray machines to see inside every single railcar that comes into the United States from Mexico. Journalist Geri Miller says this is especially amazing because the machines work "while the cars are rolling."[7] Usually they discover that the cargo does carry what was declared. Sometimes, however, they find illegal drugs or weapons. Other times they find stowaways—people hiding inside.[8]

CBP officers use radiation-detection devices to help them find weapons of mass destruction. These devices can sense the radioactive products used to make these weapons. CBP officers were recently onboard a container ship from South Korea. The officers wore small radiation-detection devices on their belts. An alarm sounded when the device detected Cobalt-60. Why did this matter? Sometimes Cobalt-60 is a product of weapons testing. But in this case, the ship's

*X-ray technology shows what is inside a truck's cargo container. CBP officers never have to enter the truck.*

This CBP officer is checking a ship's cargo for dangerous chemicals.

fire-extinguishing system needed Cobalt-60 to function. What the detector picked up was not dangerous. But it is important to know it senses things that are potentially dangerous. In three years, CBP personnel's radiation devices went off more than ten thousand times. Fortunately, they have yet to detect a nuclear weapon.[9]

CBP officers look at cargo coming into the country. But do you think it is also important for them to look at what is leaving the United States? They inspect that cargo, too. One thing they are looking for is weapons. The government needs to prevent certain weapons and technologies from getting into the hands of terrorists. They also search for money. They especially look for large amounts of cash or checks going to the Middle East. This is because the money may be used to support terrorism. Finally, they are on the lookout for drug money. In 2005, CBP officers in Laredo, Texas, came across $1.7 million inside the panels of a 2003 Honda Accord.[10]

Most CBP officers who inspect cargo work in the United States. Some do work at ports overseas, however. There they examine high-risk cargo before it is loaded on ships bound for the United States. There are CBP officers assigned to stations in the Netherlands, Singapore, Japan, South Africa, and sixteen other ports.

## What It Is Like to Work as a CBP Officer

"Exciting." "Rewarding." These are words CBP officers use to describe their job. Still, they quickly admit that "a CBP career can be tough work."[11] They say it requires mental discipline. After all, CBP officers have to remain alert for hours at a time. It can be physically tiring as well. CBP officers have to be fit. They need stamina. Remember, they have to climb aboard trucks and railroad cars and into ships' holds. Sometimes they crawl into tight spaces, searching for secret compartments. They are looking for places where criminals might have stashed weapons, drugs, or even people. CBP officers sometimes work outside on piers and airport tarmacs and railroad stations. They do not get to go inside if the weather turns nasty.

CBP officers work long hours. They put in a lot of overtime. At busy airports, officers have to work overnight, on weekends, and on holidays. Their jobs can put them under a great deal of stress. It is important for CBP officers, like Border Patrol agents, to be able to keep their cool. They must remain professional in the face of angry or frightened people. They need to think on their feet when trouble breaks out. What if they encounter a terrorist? What if they come across a dangerous weapon?

Even if the job is hard, it has great rewards. CBP officers take great pride in their work. They also receive a good salary. They start out earning between $30,000 and $35,000 per year.[12] Officers also earn generous overtime pay. CBP provides them health and life insurance and a retirement program. At some places, CBP officers have access to fitness centers and child-care programs.

## Qualifications

All CBP officers are required to be U.S. citizens and to have a valid driver's license. Applicants must be twenty-one years or older. It helps when candidates can speak another language in addition to English. CBP officers need either a college degree or three years of work

The job of a CBP officer can be stressful. These officers are making an arrest.

experience. Officers make more money if they did well academically at college or earned a graduate degree. So do people who come into CBP with specialized experience. This type of experience might include being in the military or working with imports and exports.

## Applying

CBP lists officer job openings on its Web site and at the federal government's job Web site. Sometimes CBP human-relations personnel also visit military bases and

## Forgery

According to CBP reports, CBP officers catch a fake document every five minutes, on average. Sometimes it is a forged passport. Other times it is a driver's license or a customs document.

Inspectors use magnifiers to look closely at documents. They look for signs that these items have been changed. Black lights help them spot changes made to a document. For example, the light might show that a photo has been removed and another pasted on. One common mistake forgers make is with dates. They might use an issue date that fell on a Sunday. (Government offices are closed on Sundays, so no papers would be issued on those days.) A passport issued on a holiday (such as Christmas) is also suspect. Inspectors look carefully at birth certificates with February 29 as a birth date to make sure they are from a leap year.

CBP officers send some documents to the Forensic Document Laboratory in McLean, Virginia. This lab has a huge collection of genuine documents. Officers can compare suspect documents to the real thing.[13] They can also use the State Department's official passports database.

One thing CBP officers have begun to see recently is look-alikes. In these cases, people trying to enter the United States carry genuine documents that are not theirs but once belonged to someone of their age and origin. The person in the passport photo also looks a lot like them.[14]

Governments are taking steps to end problems with passports. For example, passports may one day include computer chips encoded with physical information about a person. The chips may even include iris scans. A machine can scan a person's eye and compare it to the scan on the computer chip. It can check to see that the color and patterns of a person's eye match the passport data.

college campuses to find potential job candidates.[15] All applicants for CBP jobs take a written test. This test has four sections. The first covers reasoning skills. Another part covers writing skills. CBP officers have to be able to write solid reports. There is a section designed to see whether someone is an ethical person and has common sense. It does this by explaining a difficult situation and then asking the person to choose how to handle it. The last section is more like a survey than a test. It asks questions about a person's experience and achievements. The agency provides applicants with study guides to help them get ready for the test.

People who get high scores on this test undergo a background check and drug testing. Administrators hire from the group of applicants with the best test scores and backgrounds. Generally, it takes eight months from the time a person first applies for a job for an offer to be made.

## Training

Once hired, new CBP officers go to the Federal Law Enforcement Training Center (FLETC) in Glynco, Georgia, for twelve weeks of training. This helps them prepare for the job. They undergo physical-fitness training. They take classes in law enforcement skills and practice using firearms. They also learn to use CBP's computer system and other high-tech equipment. FLETC has a full-size port of entry setup where officers can practice observing traffic and interviewing passengers.

Once CBP officers have graduated and begin to work at a real port of entry, they have more on-the-job training. Throughout their careers, CBP officers continue to get more training and to practice their weapons skills. Continuous training and good job performance lead to promotions for CBP officers.

## A High-Tech Fingerprint Database

One tool CBP employees use is the Integrated Automated Fingerprint Identification System (IAFIS). The Federal Bureau of Investigation (FBI) maintains the IAFIS. It is the world's largest fingerprint database. In fact, it includes the prints of more than 47 million people.

Crime-scene investigators collect latent fingerprints and enter them into the IAFIS. A latent fingerprint is invisible to the eye, but it can be seen when an examiner applies dust or chemicals to a surface.

Law enforcement agents can use IAFIS twenty-four hours a day, seven days a week. CBP officers use

it to make sure people entering the country are really who they claim to be. After they scan in a print, agents can get information about a person's identity in just two hours.[16]

## Agriculture Specialists

Have you ever driven to Mexico or Canada for a vacation? Perhaps you looked out the window on your way back home. Near the U.S. border, you saw signs warning that you cannot bring most fruits and vegetables into the United States. Imported plants and produce—fruits, vegetables, and flowers—need to be inspected. Why? Sometimes they carry disease. Diseased plants can infect healthy plants. Sometimes plants are home to insects that are pests.

In the nineteenth century, tiny aphids were transported from the United States to France by mistake. These bugs thrived in the vineyards of France. During the Great French Wine Blight, almost half of France's grapevines were ruined. The aphid problem was finally brought under control, but many other dangerous insects exist. Sometimes fruits and vegetables are contaminated. Maybe they have been washed in dirty water or sprayed with insecticides. This can make people sick.

## What Do Agriculture Specialists Do?

Agriculture specialists prevent plant diseases and pests from getting into the country. They also watch out for biological weapons. These weapons use bacteria or other biological materials to make people deathly ill. At border checkpoints and ports of entry, agriculture specialists look through cargo and baggage. Produce

*An agriculture specialist carefully looks at flowers for signs of insect invaders or plant diseases.*

coming into the United States from other countries is sent for inspection at warehouses called pre-clearance stations. At the stations, specialists carefully look over fruits, vegetables, and flowers. They also look at the containers in which the produce arrives. They check for insects, insect larvae, and signs of disease.

For example, agriculture specialists might look for the brown fir longhorn beetle or the Japanese cedar longhorn beetle. Both of these insects often come into the United States on items made from wood in China. The beetles infest and kill pine trees.[17] Another danger is the false coddling moth, which can ruin citrus harvests. The Mediterranean fruit fly can damage two hundred fifty kinds of plants.

When agriculture specialists find contaminated fruit or diseased plants, they seize them. This means the plants are not sent on for sale in the United States. Agriculture specialists must disinfect or decontaminate

> The Mediterranean fruit fly can damage two hundred fifty kinds of plants.

bad produce. They kill the dangerous insects that live on the plants.

Agriculture specialists have some duties that do not involve plants. For example, they check meat by-products (including dog or cat food that contains meat) that come into the country. Some agriculture specialists collect and analyze data. They check to find out where specific diseases originate or how they seem to spread.

In just 1 year's time, CBP agriculture specialists performed 5 million cargo checks. They also inspected 1 million vehicles and talked to 81 million people who were entering the country. Their results were incredible: In all, they made 1.5 million seizures.[18]

## Qualifications

When agriculture specialist jobs become available at CBP, there are always many applicants. These jobs are difficult to get. One reason is that specialists often receive good pay. In 2006, people with experience started out at about $31,000 per year.[19]

Agriculture specialists need special skills and education. A college degree in biology or botany is

Pests can do great damage if they enter the country on plants. Agriculture specialists need a college degree in biology or botany so they can do their jobs well.

**A CBP dog sniffs out smuggled produce in someone's luggage at the airport.**

required. Other majors can also help in getting a job as an agriculture specialist. These include agricultural science, natural-resource management, and chemistry. CBP also hires people who have just one year of college, but they must have related job experience. Perhaps they have worked in pest control, or they might have worked for an environmental organization.

To be a good agriculture specialist, a person must be able to do detailed work. A specialist often has to stay attentive for hours at a time. Agriculture specialists also need to be good at keeping records. They must have great communications skills. Sometimes they need to discuss a problem with CBP scientists or other experts.[20]

## Applying

There are not as many agriculture specialists as there are Border Patrol agents and CBP officers. For this reason, the job is not advertised very often. When there are openings, they are announced on the CBP Web site. They also appear on the federal government job Web site. Interested people can fill out online applications. Like other CBP employees, applicants for agriculture specialist jobs have to undergo a background check.

## Training

To learn the skills they will need, new agriculture specialists attend the U.S. Department of Agriculture's Professional Development Center in Frederick, Maryland. But first, they spend twenty days in training at the port where they will work after graduation from the academy. They learn about the Department of Homeland Security and agencies related to their work. They receive training in defensive driving. They learn how to handle stress, because the job can be a difficult one. Finally, they receive extensive training in the use of pesticides—substances used to destroy pests.

At the Professional Development Center, the specialists go through two to three months of training. They learn inspection techniques. They take special science classes and learn about agricultural practices around the world. CBP works closely with the U.S. Department of Agriculture to train its inspection force. The center's first class graduated in the summer of 2004.

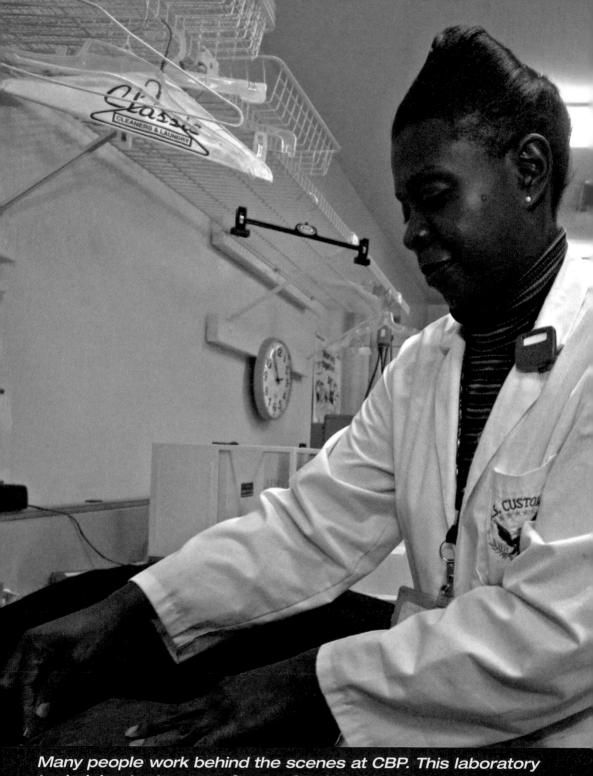

Many people work behind the scenes at CBP. This laboratory technician tests cargo from a foreign country.

# Chapter 5

# *Behind the Scenes*

Border Patrol agents, CBP officers, and agriculture specialists make up most of the CBP workforce. They also are the most visible to the public. Many more people work for the agency, however. Thousands of CBP employees work behind the scenes. Some are managers or administrators. Others are professional people with special skills. They include scientists, analysts, and import specialists. CBP has a huge support staff as well. This includes secretaries, computer technicians, and other positions. CBP could not function without people in support jobs.[1]

The public information office has a lot of support personnel. CBP employs photographers and writers who work in the agency's public-relations office. They help explain CBP's role in fighting terrorism to the media and to the American people.

### *Border Patrol Support*

Another group of CBP support personnel is the law enforcement communications assistants (LECAs). LECAs back up Border Patrol agents by providing them

*Law enforcement communications assistants (LECAs) use technology to help Border Patrol agents in the field.*

with information they need. Sometimes Border Patrol agents need a driver's license number. They might need to know if someone has a criminal record. LECAs do this kind of research using government databases. LECAs also monitor surveillance equipment.

At the communications center in Laredo, Texas, LECAs sit in front of a video wall. They watch images from forty surveillance cameras that show events as they happen. When LECAs see trouble, they check the location of the monitor. Then they send an agent to catch someone sneaking across the border, for example. To communicate with agents who cannot be reached by telephone, they use land-to-mobile radios.[2]

The position of LECA requires a high-school diploma. As with all CBP jobs, applicants must undergo a background check and take a drug test. A LECA's salary starts at about $25,000.

## CBP Scientists

Many people would enjoy the job of a CBP scientist. CBP employs 185 scientists—chemists, biologists, textile analysts, physicists, and forensic scientists.[3] CBP also employs fingerprint and DNA specialists.

CBP scientists work in several science labs. The biggest lab is in Virginia. It provides information to the people who work at CBP headquarters in Washington, D.C. There are other CBP labs in New York; Chicago; Savannah, Georgia; New Orleans; Los Angeles; and Puerto Rico. CBP even has a few mobile labs. This allows laboratory personnel to go wherever they are needed around the country.

CBP official Ira Reese described the CBP scientist job like this: "To work in a CBP lab you have to be a bit of a sleuth. The range of work is incredible."[4] CBP scientists' most important job is detecting and analyzing weapons of mass destruction and the materials used to make them. Suppose a CBP officer seizes a suspicious chemical. The scientists test the chemical to see who made it or where it came from.

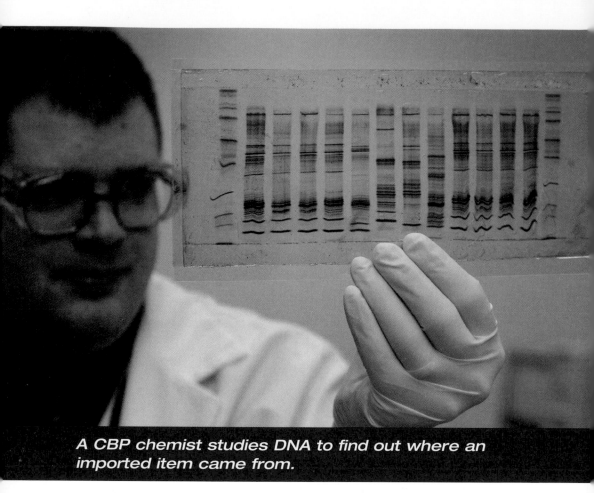

A CBP chemist studies DNA to find out where an imported item came from.

What if an agriculture specialist suspects that an importer is lying about where a shipment of plants was grown? The CBP scientists analyze the soil on the plants' roots to find the truth. And what if a Border Patrol agent stops a suspected terrorist? CBP scientists look at his or her documents to find out whether they are forgeries. CBP scientists also help determine whether containers carry bombs or drugs. They check to see if video games or perfumes are genuine or illegal knockoffs.

CBP does not employ many scientists. Competition for these jobs is tough. CBP scientists need four years of college. There are some laboratory jobs that require a doctorate degree. CBP scientists' salaries range widely according to experience and education.

## Support Jobs

Like all government agencies, CBP needs support personnel to operate effectively. The agency produces an enormous quantity of paperwork. One important job is that of the secretary, or clerk. These employees are also called administrative support people. It takes hundreds of people to help manage information for the agency. They keep its records and databases up-to-date.

Many clerks work at the agency's Washington, D.C., headquarters. The agency also has support personnel in other offices around the country. One example is the position of secretary for a Border Patrol sector office. This job includes many responsibilities. The employee takes telephone calls and greets visitors. He or she looks at mail and makes sure it gets to the right people. The person also writes letters and reports. Sometimes the employee has to go through files to gather information. The office chief needs the secretary to make travel arrangements (such as airplane, car, and hotel reservations) and to update his or her calendar.

This kind of job does not require highly specialized skills. These positions are available to a larger group of applicants. Still, applicants must be U.S. citizens. They need either one year of experience with this type of work or a degree from a business or technical school or a college.

Clerical and secretarial jobs are listed online on the federal jobs Web site. Applicants submit a resume and fill out a questionnaire. Special consideration is given to military veterans or "disabled veterans; Purple Heart recipients; spouses or mothers of a 100 percent disabled veteran; or the widows, widowers, or mothers of a deceased veteran."[5] Salaries start at $30,000.[6]

> Technical support personnel maintain CBP's extensive computer system. CBP owns other complicated electronic equipment, too. All these high-tech machines require maintenance.

Another important support job at CBP is the technical support person, or technician. Technical support personnel maintain CBP's extensive computer system. CBP owns other complicated electronic equipment, too. All these high-tech machines require maintenance. Sometimes they need upgrades. Like clerks, technical support personnel are not required to have a college degree. They may be hired if they have six months of work experience or one year at a trade or business school.

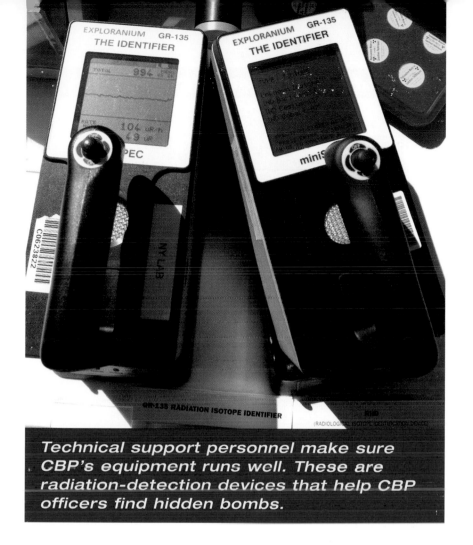

EXPLORANIUM GR-135
THE IDENTIFIER

EXPLORANIUM GR-135
THE IDENTIFIER

TOTAL 994

RATE 104 uR/h
49 uR

GR-135 RADIATION ISOTOPE IDENTIFIER

(RADIOLOGICAL ISOTOPE IDENTIFICATION DEVICE)

Technical support personnel make sure CBP's equipment runs well. These are radiation-detection devices that help CBP officers find hidden bombs.

All ports of entry have clerical and technical support personnel. Clerical and technical support personnel also work in large numbers for the agency's Information Services Office. Their tasks include collecting and managing data that can lead to the capture of terrorists.

Mission support assistants work for administrators in a particular area. Some work for the finance and budget office. Others work in procurement, meaning they acquire

## The National Targeting Center

The National Targeting Center (NTC) is a CBP office. It coordinates antiterrorism efforts. Specially trained targeters work there. Targeters are data and intelligence analysts. CBP officers and Border Patrol agents also may work at the NTC for three or four months at a time.

The public cannot be told exactly what the NTC does. It is top-secret work. We do know it acts on tips. The center gets hundreds of calls a day. These calls warn the center's personnel of suspicious activity. In response to a call, targeters might look at an importer's records. They might notice that an importer has purchased something that can be used to make drugs or weapons. Targeters might also check ships' cargo lists for suspicious items. They review bank records for huge bank deposits that might be payment for weapons. Sometimes they call law enforcement officers in other countries. On a tip, they might ask foreign customs officials to inspect a particular ship before it leaves port.[7]

supplies—everything from pencils and pens to expensive, high-tech equipment—or services for the agency. Still others work for human resources. This department handles employee hiring, payroll, and benefits.

In July 2006, a mission support assistant position opened up in the Grand Forks, North Dakota, office. Candidates needed one year of work experience. They had to be able to operate general office equipment and to type at least forty words per minute. On the job, the mission support assistant would maintain records of business transactions, buy office equipment, organize files, complete paperwork, and write reports. There were no specialized education requirements for the position. The salary range would be about $32,000 to $41,000 per year.[8]

## Some CBP Jobs and Salaries at a Glance

| Position | Starting Salary |
| --- | --- |
| Border Patrol agent | $34,000–$38,700 |
| CBP officer | $30,000–$35,000 |
| Agriculture specialist | $31,000 (need some experience) |
| Law enforcement communications assistant (LECA) | $25,000 |
| Clerical/secretarial job | $30,000 |
| Mission support assistant | Full salary range: $32,000–$41,000 |

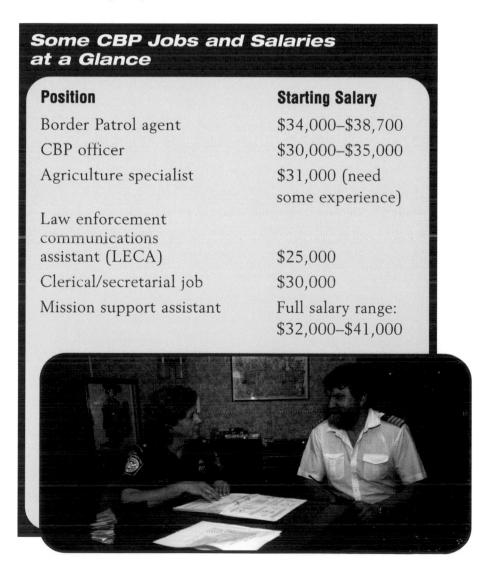

## Detector Dog Teams

Not all CBP support staff are human! Some lucky CBP employees get to spend their days working with dogs. They are part of a detector dog team. These teams are made up of a dog and a CBP officer or Border Patrol agent. Both dogs and their handlers get special training at the Canine Enforcement Training Center in Front Royal, Virginia.

Are detector dogs of just one breed? No. Teams include Labrador retrievers, golden retrievers, German shepherds, Belgian malinois, and mixed-breed dogs. Agriculture specialists use beagles as well. Many of the dogs come from animal shelters. CBP also has begun a breeding program. This will provide more dogs that are able to do the difficult work of their job. Detector dogs are between one and three years old.

Dog handlers are chosen from CBP employees who have been on the job for several years. Handlers are responsible for handling and training their dogs. They also kennel them. This means that handlers feed their dogs, prepare their beds, and make sure the animals get enough exercise—just as a pet owner would.

Dogs help CBP by detecting drugs, bombs, weapons, and money. They are even trained to sniff out hidden people. The CBP officers who work at airports, seaports, and border crossings have eight hundred dog teams. The Border Patrol has four hundred fifty more. Dogs work eight-hour days. They search aircraft, boats, train cars, baggage, cargo, mailbags, and passengers. A single dog can check

hundreds of packages in thirty minutes. They can check a vehicle in five minutes—much faster than the twenty minutes it would take a human.

In 2005, Jacko, a Belgian malinois, was named America's favorite dog hero. Every year, the Paws to Recognize Program honors service dogs. Over six years, Jacko helped the Border Patrol track down 218 people and capture almost 35,000 pounds of marijuana.[9]

CBP officers board a ship to inspect its cargo.

# Chapter 6

# *The Future*

On March 1, 2005, CBP celebrated its second birthday. Its head at the time, Commissioner Robert Bonner, looked back at everything the new agency had achieved. Creating CBP was not easy. It combined personnel from four agencies that had four different ways of doing things. Looking back, Bonner felt proud. He headed up a team of forty thousand employees. All of them were absolutely dedicated to keeping the nation safe, and they were doing a good job.

Before September 11, 2001, law enforcement agents considered fighting terrorism to be just one part of their job. Today it is one of their most important duties. CBP keeps illegal workers out of the country. It collects duties for the government. It stops drugs and other dangerous or illegal goods at our borders and ports of entry. First and foremost, however, every CBP employee works to keep terrorists and their weapons out of the country. This means *every* employee. It is the job not just of Border Patrol agents and CBP officers. It is the work of the scientists, agriculture specialists, and administrators like Commissioner Bonner. It is the responsibility of CBP support staff, including LECAs, clerks, and technicians.

CBP reports list many times when CBP workers stopped terrorists. Here are a just a few. In December 2003, a CBP officer was working in the Houston airport baggage area. He stopped a passenger from London. The officer found out that the man was on his way to Panama. He had plans to attend a terrorist meeting. In July 2004, Border Patrol officers were making routine inspections at another Texas airport. They stopped a passenger from South Africa. Something seemed to be wrong with his passport. He turned out to be a possible suspect in the bombing of a U.S. consulate. In 2004, an Irish citizen going through customs in Philadelphia was discovered to be a convicted bomber.[1]

## The Future of CBP

When Bonner stopped to reflect on CBP and its accomplishments, he said,

> Ours is not an easy job, but it is surely one of the most important jobs of any agency of the federal government. America looks to her frontline law enforcement officers—to CBP employees— to protect our homeland and our way of life. Nothing is more important, and I believe our officers, agents, and our support personnel do an outstanding job every day—24/7.[2]

Border Patrol Agent

The Border Patrol has a busy future protecting the country. This CBP officer is checking the documents of a small commercial airplane.

What does the future hold for CBP? It is certain that CBP employees will have many more innovative tools to use. CBP constantly adds new programs and comes up with new ways to use technology.

The Border Patrol will continue to come up with new ways to watch our borders. The agency hopes that it will be able to add more and more Border Patrol agents to its ranks. Many citizens want the Border

Patrol to have more of a presence on both the northern and the southern borders. This depends on the federal budget. Increasing the number of employees on an agency payroll is expensive.

In the future, CBP's use of surveillance equipment, including UAVs, will increase. One of the agency's goals is to use UAVs to create an aerial patrol. This would be especially useful in places where the border is in the wilderness.

A new program called America's Shield will help agents in many ways. It will increase surveillance of the border with electronics. It will replace aging equipment. It will provide better detectors for chemicals, explosives, and other dangerous materials. Finally, it will develop sensors that can distinguish between animals and humans.[3] This means agents will not be sent out on a false alarm if a sensor detects an animal's movement.

CBP officers also will have new and improved tools at their disposal. They will have better ways to tell whether a traveler seeking to enter the United States should be trusted. In the future, biometric technology will allow CBP officers to spend less time checking documents to see if they are real. New programs will help officers know in advance which cargo importers are planning to ship to the United States. Bonner especially looked forward to increased cooperation between the United States and other countries.

## Is CBP in Your Future?

Do you think you might want to work for CBP? Border Patrol agents feel a great deal of team spirit, and they take pride in their work. They feel great loyalty to each

It is important for CBP to cooperate with other countries. Here, Commissioner Bonner signs an agreement with the government of Dubai in the Middle East.

other. Imagine the pride Diana Dean feels, knowing that she saved the Los Angeles airport. Agents also like knowing that they help individuals while they protect the country. CBP officers feel especially proud when they catch a large drug shipment.

Another good thing about working for CBP is that federal government jobs pay relatively well. They also have good benefits, such as insurance and retirement programs. CBP does not pay its employees as much as many high-powered companies do. Still, its officers and agents make more than many other people in law enforcement. Another good thing about CBP jobs is that there are plenty of chances to advance to a higher-level position. This means higher pay, too. In addition, CBP employees qualify for career appointments. This means people are guaranteed employment. They have a high level of job security.

As with any job, there are drawbacks to working for CBP. It can be exhausting and stressful. It can even be downright dangerous. In the past, both Border Patrol agents and CBP officers have been hurt. Some have even died in the line of duty. Both agents and officers have jobs that can be difficult physically.

## A Year in the Life of CBP

In 2004, CBP employees talked to 428 million people. Some came to the United States by airplane, ship, and train. Others arrived in cars or trucks. Still others simply walked across the border. There is a bridge that carries foot traffic from Nuevo Laredo, Mexico, to Laredo, Texas.

Who were those 428 million people? Americans returning home numbered 166 million. The other 262 million came from other countries. CBP officers turned away 643,000 people who were not U.S. citizens. Most were sent home because they did not come with the right papers. Border Patrol agents also arrested more than 1 million illegal aliens.[4]

In a single year, CBP also processed 132 million imports. Working with U.S. Immigration and Customs Enforcement, CBP officers seized fake goods worth $138 million. They collected $25 billion in import duties.[5] People working for CBP seized illegal drugs 56,000 times. All together, the drugs weighed more than 2 million pounds and were worth more than $2 billion.

Many CBP employees work a lot of overtime. This can be hard on their families. Sometimes agents and officers run into difficult people. Some of these people are just regular travelers. They may dislike having to explain what they are doing. In other cases, they are dangerous criminals. Another disadvantage is that the

As with any job, there are drawbacks to working for CBP. It can be exhausting and stressful. Both agents and officers have jobs that can be difficult physically.

work can be boring. Checking documents or watching video monitors all day is not usually exciting. It is stressful knowing that an entire nation is depending on you to catch the "bad guys."

Another hard fact is that from time to time, the CBP is criticized. Citizens ask hard questions. For example, in June 2004, people in California complained about Border Patrol agents after they did some immigration sweeps to look for illegal aliens. Locals worried that the agents were using racial profiling.[6] This means stopping people because of their race or ethnic background. Many of these people

A CBP Blackhawk helicopter chases down suspects.

*Even though many different kinds of people work at CBP, the agency likes to think of itself as "one face at the border."*

had done nothing wrong and had a right to work and live in the country.

The public also found problems with a report from 2004. It said the Border Patrol did not have enough money in its budget to stop every illegal alien the agents uncovered. Agents had to let go people who were not criminals or dangerous. But these people still did not have the right to stay in the United States.[7]

Employees of all government agencies worry about their budgets, and CBP is no exception. CBP's budget for 2006 was expected to be $6.7 billion. This may seem like more money than it could possibly spend. In reality, government agencies always find they do not have enough money. Americans want CBP to do more to protect them, yet the government does not have more money to give. Sometimes CBP employees find it difficult to work with limited funds and outdated equipment. For example, the agency needs new helicopters for the Border Patrol. Without money, getting the new equipment is not possible.[8]

Many of these disadvantages can be found in every career. CBP employees would tell you that the benefits of their job far outweigh the drawbacks. CBP staff find their work rewarding. It makes them proud to know they are doing such an important job. After all, protection of the nation's borders is vital work.

## Get Ready

So now you know about CBP. If you have decided you might be interested in a CBP career, there are many things you can do to prepare for a job with the agency.

One thing you must do is stay out of trouble. CBP cannot hire anyone who has a problem with drugs or alcohol. Bad credit is another thing to avoid. This means you cannot have a lot of debt or fail to pay your bills on time. A CBP employee must never have been in serious trouble with the law. A misdemeanor (a less serious crime) might not keep you from serving. It is most important that a person not try to cover up past problems, but instead tell the truth.

Also keep in mind that you must be physically fit to become a Border Patrol agent or CBP officer. Remember, all candidates for these jobs have to be able to do many push-ups and sit-ups. Playing sports and exercising now will help keep you in top condition. That will help you land the job you want in the future.

Another thing you can do is to observe carefully what happens whenever you go through an airport or cross a national border. See how professional CBP officers have to be. They must be on guard at all times. Notice that agents also try to be friendly. After all, most visitors to the United States come for good reasons. They need to be made to feel welcome.[9] Could you strike this balance? Could you succeed at being alert and relaxed at the same time?

## The Super Bowl

Many people worry that terrorists will strike Americans at a huge public gathering. What if they planted a bomb at Disney World? What if they assassinated a president while he was being sworn into office? The Super Bowl might also be a target.

In January 2003, it was CBP's job to prevent anything from happening at the Super Bowl. In the weeks before the big game, CBP officers set up a mobile platform vehicle and cargo-inspection system. They scanned all cargo trucks that entered the football stadium.

On game day, CBP pilots manned two Cessna Citation interceptor aircraft and two UH60 Blackhawk apprehension helicopters. They made sure that no other aircraft got anywhere near the stadium. On the ground, detection systems specialists backed up the aircraft.[10] Once again, CBP employees helped keep Americans safe and secure.

Some high-school classes will prepare someone for a CBP career. All Border Patrol officers need to know Spanish, for example. Learning other languages may help as well. At some high schools, there are classes in law enforcement. Some schools teach criminal justice. These classes are great for people who want to become police officers. They are also good for people who want to work for government agencies like CBP, the Federal Bureau of Investigation (FBI), or the Central Intelligence Agency (CIA).

> Some high-school classes will prepare someone for a CBP career. All Border Patrol officers need to know Spanish, for example.

Another thing some students do is apply for CBP's Explorer Academy. Students between the ages of fourteen and twenty-one can become Explorers. First, students participate in CBP's Explorer Program, a camp where they learn what it is like to work for the agency. Then students apply to go through the more advanced Explorer Academy. The academy educates young people about specific law enforcement techniques. Many graduates of the academy go on to join CBP when they are older.

DHS and CBP officials administer the oath of office to CBP officers in Newark, New Jersey, in August 2004.

## CBP in Iraq

Most CBP personnel work in the United States, but both CBP officers and Border Patrol agents also have been to Iraq. In 2004 and 2005, they went there to help train Iraqi border police. Their aim was to make it possible for Iraqis to protect their own borders. Former CBP commissioner Robert Bonner said one of the agency's goals was to "keep saboteurs, terrorists and armaments from crossing into or out of Iraq."[11]

CBP personnel trained 2,100 Iraqi border agents. They provided them with courses on border security and human rights. They also taught them about defensive tactics, how to use weapons, and how to do vehicle searches.[12]

People who attend the Explorer Academy receive training in skills that Border Patrol agents and CBP officers need. They also get on-the-job experience. As an Explorer, you might help out with crowd control at airports or seaports. You might take part in a surveillance operation or observe boat or truck searches. Other Explorers participate in the Law Enforcement Explorer Conference. This brings together high-school students who are part of various law enforcement agencies' summer programs.

Kids who have been through the CBP Explorer Program say they gained self-confidence and discipline. They enjoyed having the chance to meet federal law enforcement officers. They also set goals for their future education. Some received college scholarships.[13]

Are you thinking about going to college? Many college courses are good choices for people who want to work for CBP. The agency often hires college graduates who majored in law enforcement. There are also many other helpful majors. These include border studies and accounting. Remember that CBP hires people with degrees in science and agriculture as well. And do not forget that good grades always pay off. Students who earn top grades enter CBP at a higher salary.

To protect your country—what could be more rewarding than that? If this sounds like something you would like to do, prepare now. In the future, you may be able to work for CBP, one of the federal government's most important law enforcement agencies!

### Chapter 1. The Millennium Bomber

1. "The Millennium Plot," *60 Minutes II*, December 26, 2001, <http://www.cbsnews.com/stories/2001/10/03/60II/main313 398.shtml> (July 26, 2005). Hal Bernton, Mike Carter, David Heath, and James Neff, "The Terrorist Within," *Seattle Times*, June 23–July 7, 2002, <http://seattletimes.nwsource.com/news/nation-world/terroristwithin/> (July 26, 2005). Jerry Seper, "Agent's Instinct Foils Attack," *Washington Times*, December 10, 2003, p. A10. "Securing Our Borders, Protecting Our Nation," *CBP Today*, January 2005, <http://www.customs.gov/xp/CustomsToday/2005/JanFeb/other/eca wards.xml> (July 26, 2005).

2. Virginia Grantier, "National Award Named After Mandan Woman," *The Bismarck Tribune*, January 6, 2005, p. 1B.

3. Seper.

4. Grantier.

5. Ibid.

6. "U.S. Customs and Border Protection's Anti-Terrorism Award Named After CBP Officers," *CBP.gov*, January 7, 2005, <http://www.cbp.gov/xp/cgov/newsroom/news_releases/archives/2005_press_releases/0012005/01072005.xml> (May 16, 2006).

7. "A Day in the Life of U.S. Customs and Border Protection," *CBP.gov*, n.d., <http://www.cbp.gov/xp/cgov/toolbox/about/accomplish/day.xml> (December 13, 2005).

### Chapter 2. A Short History of Customs and Border Protection

1. Irving H. King, *The Coast Guard Under Sail* (Annapolis,

Md.: Naval Institute Press, 1989), pp. 1–3. Carl E. Prince, *The U.S. Customs Service: A Bicentennial History* (Washington, D.C.: Department of the Treasury, U.S. Customs Service, 1989), pp. 1–5.

2. Patrick Healy and Geoff Edgers, "U.S. adjusts museum loss figures," *Boston Globe*, May 17, 2003, <http://te.verweg.com/pipermail/cpprot/2003-May/000163.html> (July 25, 2005). "FBI Top Ten Art Crimes—Iraqi Stolen and Looted Artifacts," *FBI.gov*, n.d., <http://www.fbi.gov/hq/cid/arttheft/topten/iraqi.htm> (January 3, 2006).

3. Marian L. Smith, "Overview of INS History," *U.S. Citizenship and Immigration Services*, January 20, 2006, <http://uscis.gov/graphics/aboutus/history/articles/oview.htm> (March 17, 2006).

4. "U.S. Department of Agriculture, Animal and Plant Health Inspection Service—Protecting America's Agricultural Resources," *CBP.gov*, n.d., <http://www.customs.gov/xp/cgov/toolbox/about/history/aqi_history.xml> (July 25, 2005).

5. "In Search of Al Qaeda: Teacher's Guide," *Frontline*, n.d., <http://www.pbs.org/wgbh/pages/frontline/teach/alqaeda/glossary.html> (January 3, 2006).

6. "'Shield America' against terrorism," *U.S. Customs Today*, January 2002, <http://www.cbp.gov/xp/CustomsToday/2002/January/custoday_shield_america.xml> (July 27, 2005). "The Great Krytron Caper," *Washington Report on Middle Eastern Affairs*, July 15, 1985, <http://www.washingtonreport.org/backissues/071585/850715006.html> (March 17, 2006).

7. Leslie Woolf, "Unified to Secure America's Borders," *CBP Today*, July/August 2004, <http://www.customs.gov/xp/

CustomsToday/2004/Aug/unified_secure_borders.xml> (July 25, 2005).

8. "Remarks of CBP Commissioner Robert C. Bonner International Association of the Chiefs of Police," *CBP Commissioner Messages, Speeches, and Statements Archives,* October 25, 2003, <http://www.customs.gov/xp/cgov/newsroom/commissioner/speeches_statements/archives/2003/oct252003.xml> (July 25, 2005).

9. John M. Doyle, "Hurricane Katrina response is the first test for merged Customs and Border Patrol air operation," *Aviation Week & Space Technology,* Volume 163, September 26, 2005, pp. 53–54.

10. Christiana Halsey, "CBP gives its best to assist Hurricane rescue, recovery," *CBP Today,* September/October 2005, <http://www.cbp.gov/xp/CustomsToday/2005/sep_oct/katrina_eb.xml> (March 17, 2006).

## Chapter 3. Working as a Border Patrol Agent

1. "GS-1896-5/7: Border Patrol Agent Fact Sheet," *CBP.gov,* April 19, 2005, <http://www.cbp.gov/linkhandler/cgov/careers/customs_careers/border_careers/border_patrol_factsheet.ctt/careers_bpa_fact.doc> (March 17, 2006).

2. Sandy Stokes, "Subtle nuances alert Border Patrol agents," *The Press Enterprise,* November 28, 2003, p. A01.

3. "Protecting Our Borders Against Terrorism," *CBP.gov,* n.d., <http://www.cbp.gov/xp/cgov/toolbox/about/mission/cbp.xml> (July 25, 2005).

4. "Frequently Asked Questions About Working for the Border Patrol," *CBP.gov,* n.d., <http://www.customs.gov/xp/

cgov/careers/customs_careers/border_careers/faqs_working_
for_the_usbp.xml> (July 25, 2005). "GS-1896-5/7: Border
Patrol Agent Fact Sheet."

5. "CBP BORSTAR Agents Race to Save Lives," *CBP.gov*, July
14, 2005, <http://www.customs.gov/xp/cgov/newsroom/
press_releases/07142005_3.xml#contacts> (July 25, 2005).
"BORSTAR," *CBP.gov*, June 9, 2003, <http://www.cbp.gov/
xp/cgov/border_security/border_patrol/borstar/borstar.xml>
(July 25, 2005).

6. Joe Vargo, "Eyes wide open: Temecula Border Patrol says
techniques used to ferret out smugglers and dope runners
work well for terrorist checks," *Press Enterprise*, August 18,
2003, p. B1.

7. Ibid.

8. "Border Patrol Agent [job]," *Careerbuilder.com*, n.d.,
<http://www.careerbuilder.com/JobSeeker/Jobs/JobDetails.as
px?Job_DID=J8E5RZ6FK7MVN69J8KF&cbRecursionCnt=1
&cbsid=b9a0f39b3e5e42fe8cebfe25766b1171-175445464-
tt-1> (March 17, 2006).

9. "New Residency Requirement for All CBP positions,"
*CBP.gov*, n.d., <http://www.customs.gov/xp/cgov/careers/
customs_careers/residency_req.xml> (July 27, 2005).

10. "Unmanned aerial vehicles support border security," *CBP
Today*, July/August 2004, <http://www.customs.gov/xp/
CustomsToday/2004/Aug/other/aerial_vehicles.xml> (July
27, 2005).

11. "Your Career on America's Frontline: U.S. Customs and
Border Protection Officer," *CBP.gov*, n.d, <http://www.
customs.gov/linkhandler/cgov/careers/customs_careers/officer

/cbp_officer .ctt/cbp_officer.pdf> (July 27, 2005).

12. Mitch Tobin, "Guardians of the line," *Arizona Daily Star*, November 27, 2005, <http://www.azstarnet.com/sn/printDS/104363> (March 17, 2006).

13. Ibid.

14. "Frequently Asked Questions About Working for the CBP Border Patrol."

15. "Border Patrol Agents Feel at Home on Range 3000," *PoliceOne.com*, March 5, 2004, <http://www.policeone.com/police-products/training/simulator/articles/81054/> (July 27, 2005).

### Chapter 4. The Job of a CBP Officer

1. Jason Peckenpaugh, "Instructing Inspectors," *Government Executive Magazine*, February 15, 2004, <http://www.govexec.com/features/0204/0204newsanalysis.htm> (March 17, 2006).

2. "Ports of Entry," *CBP.gov*, n.d., <http://www.customs.gov/xp/cgov/toolbox/contacts/ports/> (July 24, 2005). "Protecting Our Borders Against Terrorism." "CBP Officer FAQs," *CBP.gov*, n.d., <http://www.cbp.gov/xp/cgov/careers/customs_careers/officer/> (July 27, 2005).

3. States News Service, "Statement of Commissioner U.S. Customs and Border Protection on Homeland Security," *Dateline Washington*, March 15, 2005.

4. "Fast Reponse Team Ready for Action," *CBP Today*, September 2004, <http://www.customs.gov/xp/Customs Today/2003/september/fast_response.xml> (July 27, 2005).

5. "Baggage Surprises," *CBP Today*, July/August 2004, <http://www.customs.gov/xp/CustomsToday/2004/Aug/baggage_surprises.xml> (July 24, 2005).

6. "'Eagle' Mobile Sea Container X-Ray System," *CBP.gov*, n.d., <http://www.customs.gov/xp/cgov/newsroom/fact_sheets/fact_sheet_eagle.xml> (July 27, 2005).

7. Geri Miller, "A Border Transformed," *Business Week*, Issue #3945, August 1, 2005, pp. 44–46.

8. "Stowaway Nabbed Using High-Tech Border Equipment," *CBP.gov*, March 9, 2005, <http://www.cbp.gov/xp/cgov/newsroom/press_releases/archives/2005_press_releases/0032005/03092005_3.xml> (March 23, 2006). "Border Agency Reports First-Year Successes," *CBP.gov*, January 11, 2005, <http://www.customs.ustreas.gov/xp/cgov/newsroom/press_releases/archives/2005_press_releases/0012005/01112005.xml> (March 23, 2006).

9. Jerry Seper, "Radiation detected on ship," *Washington Times*, January 31, 2005, p. A5. States News Service, "Statement of Commissioner U.S. Customs and Border Protection on Homeland Security."

10. Rick Pauza, "Largest Currency Seizure in History for Port of Laredo," *CBP Today*, April 2005, <http://www.customs.gov/xp/CustomsToday/2005/April/largest_currency.xml> (July 27, 2005).

11. "Your Career on America's Frontline."

12. "Frequently Asked Questions About Working for the CBP Border Patrol."

13. "Keeping It Real," *CBP Today*, January/February 2004, <http://www.customs.ov/xp/CustomsToday/2004/JanFeb/ikF adePapers.xml> (March 17, 2006).

14. U.S. House of Representatives House Select Committee on Homeland Security, Testimony of C. Stewart Verdery, Jr.: "Disrupting Terrorist Travel," September 30, 2004.

15. "CBP Launches Recruiting Effort for Border Patrol Agents," *CBP.gov*, July 1, 2005, <http://www.customs.gov/xp/cgov/newsroom/press_releases/07012005.xml> (July 2, 2005).

16. "Integrated Automated Fingerprint Identification System," *FBI.gov*, n.d., <http://www.fbi.gov/hq/cjisd/iafis.htm> (July 27, 2005).

17. "USDA Suspends Importation of Wooden Craft Items from China," *CBP Today*, April 2005, <http://www.customs.gov/xp/CustomsToday/2005/April/usda_suspends.xml> (July 27, 2005).

18. "Border Agency Reports First-Year Successes."

19. "2006-GS: Incorporating the 2.10% General Schedule Increase," *Office of Personnel Management*, n.d., <http://www.opm.gov/oca/06tables/html/gs.asp> (May 15, 2006).

20. "Agricultural Workers," *Occupational Outlook Handbook*, n.d., <http://www.umsl.edu/services/govdocs/ooh20022003/ocos285.htm> (July 27, 2005).

### Chapter 5. Behind the Scenes

1. "Other Occupations," *CBP.gov*, n.d., <www.cbp.gov/xp/cgov/careers/customs _careers/occupations> (March 17, 2005).

2. "Windows on the Border," *CBP Today*, July/August 2004, <http://www.customs.gov/xp/CustomsToday/2004/Aug/other/windows_borders.xml> (July 27, 2005).

3. "It's All About Science," *CBP Today*, April 2005, <http://www.customs.gov/xp/CustomsToday/2005/April/about_science.xml> (July 27, 2005). "Organization and Operations, Laboratories and Scientific Services," *CBP.gov*, n.d., <http://www.customs.gov/xp/cgov/import/operations_support/labs_scientific_svcs/org_and_operations.xml> (July 27, 2005).

4. "It's All About Science."

5. "[CBP Secretary job description]," *USAJOBS*, July 2005, <http://jobsearch.usajobs.opm.gov/getjob.asp?JobID=31954350&brd=3876&AVSDM=2005%2D07%2D19+00%3A01%3A00&q=cbp&sort=rv&vw=d&Logo=0&FedPub=Y&FedEmp=N&SUBMIT1.x=55&SUBMIT1.y=15&ss=0&TabNum=3&rc=3> (July 25, 2005).

6. Ibid.

7. "A New Team Against Terorrism," *CBP Today*, June/July 2003, <http://www.customs.gov/xp/CustomsToday/2003/june_july/ntcfinal.xml> (July 27, 2005). "National Targeting Center keeps terrorism at bay," *CBP Today*, March 2005, <http://www.customs.gov/xp/CustomsToday/2005/March/ntc.xml> (July 27, 2005).

8. "Mission Support Assistant (OA) Job Announcement WAS-117691-CJE," *USAJobs*, July–August 2006, <http://jobsearch.usajobs.opm.gov/getjob.asp?JobID=46051546&jbf574=HSBD&brd=3876&AVSDM=2006%2D07%2D27+00%3A01%3A01&vw=d&Logo=0&FedPub=Y&caller=%2Fa9custom%2Easp&FedEmp=N&SUBMIT1.x=76&SUBMIT1.y=14&ss=0&SUBMIT1=Search+for+Jobs&TabNum=1&rc=5> (July 27, 2006).

9. "Canines—Frequently Asked Questions," *CBP.gov*, n.d., <http://www.customs.gov/xp/cgov/border_security/canines/faq.xml> (July 27, 2005). "Canine Training History," *CBP.gov*, n.d., <http://www.customs.gov/xp/cgov/border_security/canines/canine_training_history.xml> (July 27, 2005).

### Chapter 6. The Future

1. "Border Agency Reports First-Year Successes," *CBP.gov*, January 11, 2005, <http://www.customs.ustreas.gov/xp/cgov/newsroom/press_releases/archives/2005_press_releases/0012005/01112005.xml> (March 23, 2006).

2. Robert Bonner, "Looking Toward the Future," *CBP Today*, March 2005, <http://www.customs.gov/xp/CustomsToday/2005/March/commissioner.xml> (July 27, 2005).

3. "Border guards eye surveillance," *FCW.com*, August 2, 2004, <http://www.fcw.com/fcw/articles/2004/0802/web-border-08-05-04.asp> (July 27, 2005).

4. State News Service, "Fact Sheet: U.S. Department of Homeland Security 2004 Year End Review," December 31, 2004.

5. U. S. House of Representatives Appropriations Committee, Subcommittee on Homeland Security. Testimony by CBP commissioner Robert C. Bonner: "Fiscal 2005 Appropriations: Homeland Security," March 25, 2004.

6. Douglas Quan, "Demonstrators Gather at Temecula Station," *Press-Enterprise*, June 20, 2004, p. B4. U. S. House of Representatives Judiciary Committee. Testimony of the Border Control Council: "Dual Mission of Immigrant and Border Security Agencies," May 8, 2005.

7. Lisa Myers, "Busted budgets on the border," *MSNBC*, July 26, 2004, <http://msnbc.msc.com/id/4962320/> (March 20, 2005).

8. States News Service, "Statement of Commissioner U.S. Customs and Border Protection on Homeland Security," *Dateline Washington*, March 15, 2005.

9. Jerry Seper, "Border Agents Put on Happy Face," *The Washington Times*, August 27, 2004, <http://washington times.com/national/20040827-121044-6690r.htm> (March 23, 2006).

10. "MVP of Superbowl XXXVII," *Customs Today*, March 2003, <http://www.cbp.gov/xp/CustomsToday/2003/March/superbowl.xml> (July 27, 2005).

11. "U.S. Customs and Border Protection Team Helps Secure Iraq's Borders," *CBP.gov*, February 1, 2005, <http://www.customs.ustreas.gov/xp/cgov/newsroom/press_releases/archives/2005_press_releases/0022005/02012005_4.xml> (March 23, 2006).

12. States News Service.

13. "Be an Explorer," *CBP.gov*, n.d., <http://www.cbp.gov/xp/cgov/careers/customs_careers/occupations/explorer_program/explorer.xml> (July 27, 2005).

**alien**—Any person in a country who is not a citizen of that country. An illegal alien is someone who is in a country without the permission of that country's government.

**biometric technology**—Equipment that uses fingerprints or facial features to verify that a person is who he or she claims to be. Such information may allow a person to enter a location or perform a certain activity, such as use a credit card.

**border**—A boundary line; a line dividing two nations.

**candidate**—A person who seeks a job or other position, such as an elected office.

**checkpoints**—Places where vehicles are stopped by border officials.

**consulate**—The office or residence of a government in a country outside its borders.

**customs**—Money (such as duties or tolls) that a government collects for imports or exports. The agency in charge of collecting these funds is also referred to by this name.

**declare**—To state something formally or officially. When people enter a country, they must declare certain items they bring with them.

**deport**—To force a person to leave. When aliens are deported, they are sent back to their homeland.

Border Patrol Agent

**detain**—To hold back or keep someone from going ahead.

**duty**—A special tax paid on goods brought into a country.

**exports**—Goods leaving one country to be sold in another.

**forensic scientists**—Scientists with special knowledge, such as medical training, who conduct work that will be used in a court of law.

**forgery**—A purposely created fake object, such as a document.

**hijackers**—People who illegally take control of an airplane, boat, or other vehicle.

**immigrants**—People who leave one country to live in another.

**imports**—Foreign goods entering a country to be sold.

**informant**—A person who provides information, often about illegal activity.

**intelligence**—Information about an enemy or a suspicious person.

**iris**—The round, colored part of an eye.

**knockoffs**—Copies or imitations of popular or expensive objects.

**law enforcement**—A group or person that makes sure laws are obeyed.

**passport**—An official document issued by a nation's government that allows people to travel to different countries.

**pesticides**—Chemicals that kill bugs on plants.

**pirated**—Copied from a legitimate item, such as a video game or DVD, without the consent of the rightful owner of the material.

**ports of entry**—Government-run posts where people and goods coming in from another country are checked.

**rappelling**—Letting oneself down a wall or cliff by using a special set of ropes.

**seize**—To take away by force or law.

**surveillance**—Watching over a person, group, or location.

**terrorist**—A person who uses force or violence to try to overthrow a government or disrupt a society.

**verify**—To confirm or make sure of the truth.

**visa**—A document that allows a passport holder to enter a country for a specific purpose such as work or study. It allows a person to stay for a set period of time. A visa is issued by the country the person will visit.

## Books

Campbell, Geoffrey. *A Vulnerable America: An Overview of National Security.* San Diego, Calif.: Lucent Books, 2004.

Cassedy, Patrice. *Law Enforcement: Careers for the Twenty-First Century.* San Diego, Calif.: Lucent Books, 2002.

Stewart, Gail B. *Defending the Borders: The Role of Border and Immigration Control.* San Diego, Calif.: Lucent Books, 2004.

Stinchcomb, James. *Opportunities in Law Enforcement and Criminal Justice Careers.* Chicago: VGM Career Horizons, 1998.

## Internet Addresses

CBP Web site
&lt;http://www.cbp.gov&gt;

CBP Careers Spotlight
&lt;http://www.cbp.gov/xp/cgov/careers/&gt;

CBP Explorer Program
&lt;http://www.cbp.gov/xp/cgov/careers/customs_careers/explorer_program/explorer.xml&gt;

Customs Service, 4, 12, 17–20, 27, 28

**D**

Dean, Diana, 5–8, 10, 13

Department of Agriculture, 17, 24–25, 27, 32, 81

Department of Homeland Security (DHS), 12, 31–32, 35, 81

dogs, use of, 40, 92–93

**E**

Ellis Island, 22

Explorer Academy, 108, 111

**F**

forgery, 38, 72–73, 86

**H**

Homeland Security Act, 31

**I**

illegal aliens, 12, 14, 22, 24, 37, 38–39, 41, 44–45, 46, 47, 51, 55, 101, 102, 105

immigration, history of, 20, 22–24

Immigration Act, 20

Immigration and Naturalization Service, 17, 22, 24, 27, 32

Immigration Service, 20, 22

import duties, 6, 12, 14, 17–20, 21, 61, 95, 101

Integrated Automated Fingerprint Identification System (IAFIS), 75

**J**

jobs, types of, 14, 33–34, 59, 83–93

**L**

law enforcement communications assistant, 42, 83–85, 96

legislation
Homeland Security Act, 31
Immigration Act, 20
Plant Quarantine Act, 25

**M**

Melendez-Perez, Jose, 13